Don Turner
10-99

AT THE
CROSSROADS
OF
HOPE

A priest's inner (city) journey

by Don Farnan

AT THE CROSSROADS OF HOPE is published by
Mariposa Press, Kansas City, MO

Printed in the United States of America

The stories contained herein are based upon fictional characters and not on
actual events. Any resemblance to real persons or situations is strictly
coincidental.

ISBN   0-9668197-0-5
LCCN   98-88548

Layout Design by Mary O'Meara
Cover Photograph by Vanessa Chafen

Special thanks to those in the Greater Kansas City area who, in their search for
God or fulfillment, have gone outside of themselves and their comfort zones to
reach out to less fortunate others.

Foreword

I have written this story primarily to raise interest in our inner cities and to encourage us to transform that interest into active ministry. I think that in some mysterious way, what's at the heart of our urban core is also at the heart of our Christian faith. Christ's preferential option for the poor should beckon us to recognize that those who dwell here are our sisters and our brothers. I am proud to be part of a church that tries to do its part to make life better for those in need.

Secondarily, I have written it to encourage those who seek spiritual lifestyles and religious vocations. Herein, I look at one man's public role as a priest, his personal longings and fears, and his inner search to attain union with God. Intending to make a positive difference in others' lives, he deals with tensions in these public, private and interior worlds in which he dwells.

By attending to secular concerns more than sacred ones, grappling with relationships that both energize and drain him, and administering grace-filled Sacraments that seem to have lost relevance for his time and location, he is able to discover a spiritual domain within.

Though these specific issues may not affect the vocations of all religious workers, they are indicative of the issues that guide our work. As individuals we are imperfect, as are the communities and institutions within which we function, but God calls us to always do better, to always go deeper, and to always show respect for the circumstances of the paths we travel.

Sometimes the discrepancies that exist between different spiritual, cultural, and environmental pathways, even though they may be close in proximity or belief-system, seem to be as

wide as the chasm between our imperfection and Christ's call
for us "to be perfected as my heavenly Father is perfect." I
hope this book helps its readers move toward the way of
perfection by encouraging them to grapple with personal
spiritual struggles.

You can bet that we fall many times along the journey as
we discern how to hear God's call and discover how to follow
God's way. But if we uncover within ourselves enough reason,
courage and faith to get back up each time we do, we might
just find ourselves standing at the crossroads of hope – a good
place to be.

Contents

BOOK 1: *Just Bad Luck*

Chapter 1 An Uphill Climb 5
Chapter 2 Food For Bodies, Nourishment For Souls .. 16
Chapter 3 Simons Says 26
Chapter 4 Sister Mary Ellen's "Gift from God" 44
Chapter 5 Rodney's Fate 52
Chapter 6 The Devil Lucifer 61
Chapter 7 All Alone in Darkness 79

BOOK 2: *In Search of A Dream*

Chapter 1 From Baptism into Life 87
Chapter 2 The Dream 92
Chapter 3 The House Mates 106
Chapter 4 Mary Kate's Journey 112
Chapter 5 The Sacraments of Vocation 122
Chapter 6 Dream Revisited 131
Chapter 7 On Feeding & Anointing the Sick 144

BOOK 3: *Wild Grapes*

Chapter 1 On Eucharist: Blood Poured Out 159
Chapter 2 Vincent's Hope and Confirmation 169
Chapter 3 The Table of Our Priestly Service 176
Chapter 4 On Reconciliation 194
Chapter 5 The Road That Lies Ahead 206
Chapter 6 Moving On 214
Chapter 7 Growing Up 223
Chapter 8 Alone Never Again 231

AT THE
CROSSROADS
OF
HOPE

BOOK 1

Just Bad Luck

"The rain to the wind said,
'you push and I'll pelt.'
They smote the garden bed
that the flowers actually knelt,
and lay lodged – though not dead.
I know how the flowers felt."

– Robert Frost

An Uphill Climb

1

It's commonly accepted that good luck occurs whenever preparation and opportunity intersect.

I guess when it comes to bad luck the opposite must be true; there's a lack of preparation and a lack of opportunity. It seems like everyone around here has been having some of this bad luck lately.

"Here" is where I live, the inner city, a place where most people don't prepare for much of anything, a place where we don't often recognize opportunity, a place where, perhaps, we're just undergoing the trials of some bad luck.

It certainly seemed like bad luck to Reaundra Jenkins as she walked along her mother's side in the middle of 27th Street, trying to shield her face from the lashing wind. The girl wished that she could have gone to school on this particular winter day, if you can believe that. She is in the sixth grade, a tough grade for her, a grade in which her peers are noticeably mean to one another. She, too, feels the impact of snide remarks, dirty looks, ugly rumors, and malicious insults.

Like many of the other students in her class, Reaundra is becoming self-conscious about how she looks and what she says and does and even thinks. Even though she believes that her skin is too dark and her clothes are too shabby, and even though she is bigger than most of the boys (and girls) her age and gets reminded of it nearly every day, Reaundra would still have rather been with her classmates at this moment. At least with them, she would have been warm and she would have felt safe – she feels safe at school most of the time. And besides that, school is the happiest part of her life. She enjoys learning about the things that are put before her.

But her mother wouldn't permit her to go to school on this particular day because her mother needed her help. The two of them were on their way to the church to get some groceries. They had to walk six and a half blocks; the last two seemed to Reaundra to go straight up hill.

At her school, she was reading Dr. King's speech about going to the mountaintop. She envisioned those prodigious hilltops of New Hampshire and those mighty mountains of New York and those heightening Alleghenies of Pennsylvania. She considered those snow-capped Rockies of Colorado and those curvaceous slopes of California. She imagined what it must be like to climb that Stone Mountain of Georgia or that Lookout Mountain of Tennessee, even those hills and molehills of Mississippi. Her own state of residence didn't get mentioned, which led her to believe that the hill to the church wasn't so steep compared with what some people had to contend. She had never seen the Rockies of Colorado or the molehills of Mississippi, but she was glad, nonetheless, that she didn't live in those other states.

Her mother needed her today to carry some of the bags or boxes down the hill and up another that led back to their home.

At the church's food pantry, the clients who qualify for assistance never know what food they'll receive, or how much they'll get, or what kind of containers the volunteer workers at the pantry will find to put the groceries in so that the clients can manage to get them home.

As the mother and daughter walked, they passed the small houses – some boarded up and abandoned, others with home-made security measures and occupied. They passed a discarded couch and abused kitchen appliances that had been tossed into a front yard, broken pieces spilling into the street. A dog was scratching open a trash bag in search of its daily nourishment.

The child wondered what her mother was thinking because it looked to her as if she had a lot on her mind. Reaundra determined that her mother had good reason to be overburdened with worries. No water flowed from the faucet in the bathroom when the girl turned the knob this morning. She didn't know if it had been turned off or if the pipes were frozen. Though she refrained from mentioning the water situation, she couldn't hold back about the cold. She thought about the ice that had formed on the inside glass of the window on their upstairs landing.

"Mama, do ya think Sister's gonna pay our bill so the gas company won't cut off our heat?" Reaundra asked her mother.

The girl had overheard her mother on the phone discussing their enormous bill from the Gas & Energy Company.

"I don't know, baby. I hope she can help us out some," came the reply.

The girl's mother hadn't asked for assistance from the church in nearly ten months. She thought that Sister Mary Ellen, the manager of the food pantry, would view her abstinence from begging as a sign of self-reliance worthy of favor today.

They moved briskly against the cold January wind. To Reaundra, their walk in the low-lying fog that surrounded them was almost spooky. Most of the way, she held on to her mother's hand. She tried to be brave because she was certain that another worry on her mother's mind had to do with the children who they had just left behind at the house they rent. The girl thought that her younger siblings should be okay as long as they sit in front of the TV.

"I sure hope them kids don't do nothin' stupid while we're gone," she mumbled aloud.

Reaundra recalled what happened one day last spring when a neighbor girl, Tiara, who lived two houses away, was supposed to stay at home and take care of herself. A man came to her door that afternoon and talked to her for a long time through the two doors that separated them, the inside wood door and the outside screen door. The man said that he was her mom's boyfriend's brother and he needed inside the house to get something that his brother forgot to give him. After she talked with him for what seemed to her a much longer time than most adults talk to kids, and after he sounded convincingly legitimate and sincere, Tiara let him in. She was only five and a half, but in our neighborhood that's old enough to know better.

The man came in, all right, and so did several others. Little Tiara was scared, but she didn't scream – not until just before she got hit, that is. Poor Tiara. She realized immediately that she had made a mistake, but she didn't know how to undo it and she feared the consequences of her bad judgment. Reaundra's mother spoke with her own brood several times last spring about how making mistakes leads to suffering consequences.

"Why didn't Tiara call for help when those bad guys broke into her house?" the girl asked her mother.

Saundra Mae, Reaundra's mother, was patient with her daughter, even though she didn't like the current topic of conversation.

"First of all, they didn't break in. She broke down and let 'em in. Second of all, I don't know. But her mama said she froze." After a brief pause she continued. "Even if she could get to a phone, she couldn't call her mama 'cuz she didn't know where her mama was. That's why I always tell you where I'm goin'. She couldn't call the neighbors 'cuz she didn't know our numbers. That's why I taught you how to call Auntie Lou and

Ms. Bodreaux usin' just one number. She couldn't call nine-one-one 'cuz, like everybody 'round us knows, they never get there till the damage is done." Then she added, though based on nothing substantial, nothing but hope, "That kinda thing's not gonna happen to you."

When Tiara ran out of potential options in the face of her intruders, she just slid down in the corner of the living room and wet herself. When her mother did return home, she discovered that the house had been robbed and her child, as the girl's mother described it, "was actin' crazy, still screamin' and cryin'." All the neighbors thought it was a damn shame that no one heard her cries for help.

"Mama, is it true they knocked her out with a gun?"

"She said she didn't remember what happened. Maybe she just passed out. All I know is, when she woke up, she was still pretty scared so she musta started cryin' and actin' crazy again, 'cuz that's how it was when her mama got home and took her to the hospital."

"She's lucky to be alive, ain't she?"

"I don't know, chile," her mother responded calmly. "That's for God to decide." She touched the bottom of her lip and tore off a piece of chapped skin from it. It bled. Without pausing, she added, "It's too cold for talkin'. Let's move along." They weren't yet halfway to their destination.

The neighbors never did hear if that was her mom's boyfriend's brother or not.

Ms. Saundra Mae Jenkins might have already been thinking about some of these things that her daughter brought to their conversation, but, if she was, they were only in the back of her mind. In the front of her mind was the concern of how she and her children would make it through the month of January. She experienced a similar concern in December; she would experience it again in February.

Not only was the woman cold. She was also frustrated by her

9

poverty, weakened by her hunger and anxious about her appointment with Sister Mary Ellen. She was relying on the nun to help her sort through the concerns that were weighing on her mind. She went over them in her head.

"It used to be if you just got through the month you'd get some more money at the start of the next month," she thought to herself. "But since the government started reformin' the welfare, it's got us all confused. Welfare reform seems like a bad thing for all of us that's poor. Not many food stamps are given out these days – too many papers to fill out to get 'em. Utility bills are sky-rocketin'. Those that used to make it by can't but barely make it. Those that barely made it b'fore can't make it at all no more."

Yes, she did, indeed, have a lot on her mind as she grabbed her daughter's hand and picked up the pace for the remainder of their walk through the freezing, foggy weather that accompanied them to the church. She tasted the blood on her lip as she thirsted for a different existence.

As you may have guessed already, Ms. Jenkins named her daughter after herself. But like many young black mothers, she wanted her child, as well as her child's name, to be unique. So she tossed out the 'S' and put an 'RE' in its place, sort of like REpeat or REproduce. Saundra added the M-a-e part to her own name later to make it more unique too. Being unique is important.

As they began to ascend the big incline two blocks from the church, "Aundra the Second" began thinking about something else all together, something she didn't like to think about. She was hoping that D.L. wouldn't see them walking by, for they were walking onto his block. She knew that he wouldn't be in school this day simply because he didn't have a school in which to be. He wasn't much older than Reaundra, maybe a couple of

10

years. She wasn't sure if he ever was in a school or if he got kicked out of it for causing too much trouble. She concluded that he probably cussed out a teacher or started a fire or used his gun to threaten someone because that is what she saw him do around the neighborhood.

"Who can blame him?" she had heard Ms. Bodreaux ask her mother without intending the other woman to respond before she, herself, could. "That's the way he's been raised."

In the middle of the street, directly in front of D.L.'s house, there was a patch of ice which Reaundra didn't see. When she slipped on it and fell to the asphalt, her mother, who hadn't let go of her hand, quickly picked her child up, embraced her, and continued moving on. Though a bit frightened and embarrassed, Reaundra said nothing. As the two hurriedly made their way to the end of D.L.'s block, the child realized that nobody would be coming out to harass them. The fog that loomed made it too dark to see clearly from the house to the street and the wind chill, alone, would keep any sensible person inside for this entire day. Besides, reasoned the girl, it's still before noon. D.L. rarely woke up this early.

Reaundra hoped that the weather conditions wouldn't change much until after they made their way back down the hill with their groceries. That would be in about half an hour. She hoped that they wouldn't run into any more bad luck today.

Adrian's gang, the gang ruling over the blocks that surround the church, lured D.L. into their ring many years ago. Their gang's territory contains piles of trash and debris that litter the yards and streets, iron bars on the windows of most buildings, and the continual noise of sirens in the air. There is neglect in city services and lack of interest by residents, which allowed the sewage drains to be backed up, the street lights to be broken, and the traffic signs to be in disrepair. It's where they all grew up. By an early age, they could distinguish the siren sounds for fire trucks, ambulances and police vehicles.

And they know the houses in their kingdom. Adrian and his gang first used D.L. when they got into tight spots. I mean that literally. When they were breaking into houses where they couldn't fit through the small spaces available to them, D.L. would help them out by volunteering to break and enter on their behalf. He was happy to do it.

Reaundra and her older brother once witnessed him squeeze through a tiny window pane in the basement of a house near their own, then unlock and open the window so that Adrian could also gain access. Back then, he bragged to Reaundra's brother that he'd usually let his friends in right through the front doors of houses. For D.L., front door entry symbolizes some kind of master claim over the conquered domain.

Adrian and his gang treated their little friend quite well. They gave him money for each break-in. They let him hang out with them. He caught on quickly and started to enjoy the work, and the pay. He was only about five or six when he began keeping their company. He went just about wherever they went. When he got older, they gave him other jobs. Those of us who lived in the neighborhood often saw him playing on the street corners. His job was to pretend to play while he watched for cops and other suspicious persons coming near their centers of drug activity. He carried a cell-phone to keep his friends and mentors informed of leery-looking traffic. This gang who cared for him taught him how to shoot guns, smoke crack and insult girls – all before he was nine years old. He must have been good at what he did for them, too, because the older gang members welcomed him eagerly and he kept getting promoted within their ranks.

Adrian and his friends were more of a family to him than his own family. That's probably why most of these boys join gangs. They want to belong to a family. With and for each other, they form a family unit. Their domicile is any abandoned house in the area, and they have access to all of them. Their backyards are the streets themselves. They are very much at home in their backyard, and they do not condone trespassers. It threatens the welfare of their family.

D.L.'s family of origin wasn't of much importance to him compared with his gang family, even though there is a plethora of family members residing at the house in which he lives. On one of her many visits to the Jenkins' rental house, Ms. Bodreaux, a friend of Saundra Mae, had informed her, in the presence of her children, all about D.L.'s household.

"Ms. Jenkins, I've been knowin' that boy's grandpa for years now. He tole me D.L.'s mama had the boy when she was thirteen. Too young to be bringin' home a baby, if you ask me."

No one ever asked her.

Her visits typically consist of several cups of coffee and several bits of gossip. She always speaks rapidly, as though the words can't wait to be aired. She enters many kitchens in our neighborhood to spout off, which has earned her the nickname, "old-crow Bodreaux."

Without much thought, Saundra Mae responded, "that's about how old D.L. is now."

"Yeah, and already he's the one runnin' their house," added Ms. Bodreaux.

The Jenkins were aware that D.L.'s mother doesn't stay at that house much, even though it is her house, too. And the old grandpa, who Ms. Bodreaux knew, doesn't have much say in what happens there.

"The ole fart's usually drunk," she offered. "His wife left him, and left all her kids behind with him, too."

The old drunken grandpa has a brother who they call "Deek." Deek stays in the same house. So do a lot of D.L.'s aunties and a bunch of little kids who are children of those aunties. Some are his own younger siblings or half-siblings, too.

Saundra Mae responded to Ms. Bodreaux, though it seemed like she was talking only to herself.

"Nobody in that house talks too nice to nobody else. No wonder D.L. came by his current ways; he didn't learn nothin' good from his real family."

"But don't think he learned nothin' good from his gang family, neither. 'Cept they sure did help him expand his vocabulary. Whoa, that chile can cuss! And don't care who he's talkin' to neither..."

While Ms. Bodreaux went on about the young boy's filthy mouth, Saundra Mae was quiet and pensive. She had been the victim of his verbal rage more than once.

It started many years ago, when she decided not to allow her children to play with him, which made him very mad. Back then, before Reaundra was even old enough to go to school, D.L. came over to the Jenkins' place to play with Ronald, who was the girl's older brother. Saundra Mae was listening from the kitchen while the children played in the backyard. She heard D.L. cussing and coaching her son to cuss, so she went outside and sent the visitor home.

She tuned back in to Ms. Bodreaux's words.

"...But I guess I don't need to tell you about his defilin' mouth. He's been downright nasty to you and your daughter. But you can still be glad it didn't work when he tried to get Ronal' to turn against you. I swear that D.L.'s got a demon in him, probly lots of 'em. I think it's a shame that that hood broke in here and stole the necklace you loved and all your other jewelry, not to mention the money you was savin' to give your kids a decent education. The police didn't even try to get it back for you. It's like they didn't b'lieve your theory."

Ms. Jenkins' voice was barely audible, and her words were slow compared to Ms. Bodreaux's. "They couldn't prove it was him. He got rid of it all too quick for me to prove anything."

Reaundra's recollection of that scene occupied her mind until they arrived at the church's pantry door. She realized that her mother was afraid of D.L., even though the woman wouldn't admit

14

it. The girl knew that most decent people were afraid of him, or at least they didn't like him.

Reaundra knew that the priest, at whose church door they now stood, fit into the latter category. She thought it odd, because the priest was supposed to like everybody. Nonetheless, she knew that the church still gives food to D.L.'s household when they need it. The young girl reasoned that whether the church's leaders like certain people or not, they will help them in desperate times anyway. Though she agreed with that philosophy, she still wondered about the priest.

The priest who caused her wonder is me.

Food For Bodies,
Nourishment For Souls

2

I, Father Thomas Hartigan, pastor of St. Peter Claver Church, encounter many people who deserve to be helped, many people in need. I also encounter a few people I don't like. That's because they are unlikeable. But as the girl's thoughts suggest, I should try to find a way to like everyone.

We all know that it's easy to like the beautiful, the intelligent, the wealthy, the successful and the generous. But it doesn't seem that there are enough people who are going out of their way to like the ugly ones, the stupid ones, the poor ones, the failures, the forgotten and rejected ones who come to the doors of our church for emergency assistance. They are the ones who don't have anything to give in return except the opportunity for us to help them.

And that is their gift, really. At least that's what I keep telling myself. I keep telling myself that the less fortunate give us the opportunity to actualize the faith that we verbally profess. It is as Flannery O'Connor once wrote, "we'll finally realize we are

16

Christians when we stop thinking about ourselves and start thinking about others." With all of those on my list to like and to feed, I have sacrificed the immoral ones to my shorter list of "unlikeables."

This is my story – three stories really. The first is about my work, the second is about my priesthood, and the third is about my church, the Catholic Church. Mine is a story about sacraments and about how sometimes dull and ordinary lives, like my own, can become sacramentally graced by searching for God.

This story looks into the three lives that we each lead – public life, private life and interior life – captured in the course of a year or, from my perspective, in the course of a moment.

The Reverend Johnny Ray Youngblood once stated in Samuel Freedman's book, *Upon This Rock*, that we church leaders are really "nothing more than beggars telling other beggars where they might find some bread." As you search through your own vocation, lifestyle and belief system – your own story – I hope that you will somehow find nourishment in the bread of life.

As Sister Mary Ellen often reminds those of us who work at St. Peter Claver: "Bread for ourselves is a material thing, but bread for others is a spiritual thing." Of course, we all rejoice constantly around here because we're given plenty of opportunities to be more spiritual each and every day.

Though I am the pastor, Sister Mary Ellen is the leader of our community. I may possess some institutional authority in our hierarchical system, but she wields the power among the people and carries their respect. She works hard to serve them and to give them the dignity they deserve as human beings made in the image and likeness of God. She provides an example of charity and holiness for all who know her.

One of her best volunteers in the pantry is Ms. Dorthea Smith. Dorthea is here every Thursday. She is the one who opened the

17

basement door for Saundra Mae Jenkins and her young girl on this cold, cloudy day that shrouded my world – a Thursday. She could tell that the pair was freezing with her initial glance. They didn't even really give her the chance to open the door for them. They just sort of pushed it when they heard movement on the other side, as the volunteer was unlocking it.

"We's freezin'," Ms. Jenkins breathed out. It was both a scream and a hushed whisper at the same time, while she moved her daughter and herself away from the door. "We pushed the bell three times."

Dorthea mumbled her first response apologetically, "I must notta heard the first two," and then recovered quickly to appear hospitable, with the situation under control. In a strong voice she continued, "Well, get in here and warm yourselves up."

Though it was rather cold inside too, Dorthea knew that it would feel warm to these two after their walk through the heart of winter. She was embarrassed that they had to stand still in the cold so long, while she found her way to the door. She is an old lady and simply can't move as fast as she prefers. In her quick brush with the out-of-doors, she saw her own breath. Then she stepped outside in a spirit of humility where she spied me getting out of my car. As the Jenkins' pushed their way past her, Dorthea looked at me looking back toward them.

To her, and to many of our volunteers, I seem to always be getting in or getting out, always coming here or going there, rushing to say Masses or sometimes to teach classes. But they are glad that each day I take time to stop down at the food pantry, even though that is usually a rush job, too.

"Maybe Father or somebody else can drive you home with your boxes after this," Dorthea suggested to the mother and daughter in the most congenial manner she could muster. She hoped that her idea would help them to forgive her for not hearing the doorbell those first times, causing them to stand outside a little longer than they had planned.

"I'm gonna get you some coffee," Dorthea announced with a smile as she exited to the pantry which contained a coffee maker.

Though they might remain cold for the rest of the day, they wouldn't remain hungry. Their boxes of food were already packed and ready to go: a family of four, one adult and three children. Ronald is no longer with them and his name was crossed from their pantry file card. But I'll tell you about his parting later in the story.

Sister Mary Ellen gets to work early each weekday morning and takes all the calls for food and other kinds of assistance during the morning hours. Once they arrive at the pantry and get settled between eleven o'clock and noon, the volunteers put the orders together, usually in boxes.

But on this particular day, Dorthea was the only volunteer who showed up, besides Rodney. The others stayed at home due to the cold. Like Dorthea, they are mostly old, retired people who want to do something worthwhile with their time. On this Thursday, Dorthea and Sister worked together preparing the boxes for those brave enough or desperate enough to venture out.

Rodney was venturing out; he was on a "bread run." One of the grocery stores across town from us donates its extra bread and many other bread items, like donuts and bagels, to our pantry once it determines that they probably won't sell in the store. Two or three times each week, Rod goes and picks up those bread products using Sister's old station wagon. It was reliable on days like this one.

To and from the grocery store is the only place he drives. Rod doesn't have a car, but Sister helped him get his driver's license. He lives only a few blocks from the church in a shabby, dilapidated apartment building which I'd be leery about entering. It looks rather dangerous, with all sorts of shady-looking characters hanging around it at all hours. He grew up close by and even went to the church's elementary school, when it still had an elementary school. That would be about thirty years ago. Rod is probably forty or forty-five now.

As Dorthea said to Sister and me, "he's a good boy, but he don't think right. I don't suppose he's mentally retarded, but he must be some kind of retarded." Rod had been culturally deprived for sure. He doesn't possess many social skills. And he is generally afraid of people.

He suffered a string of bad luck, himself. His mother took care of him until she passed away, nearly ten years ago. He has an older brother, but his brother lives with his own family half way around the world. Because he's got his own life, he doesn't have a whole lot to do with Rod. He found his own life when he was in Vietnam. It's hard to believe that that war served as a threshold to a better life for some of our nation's soldiers. It did for Rod's brother. That was where he met his wife, but it's not where they ended up; they're living in France. The last time that Rodney's brother visited him was for their mother's funeral.

Sister Mary Ellen gets an envelope from France each month in the mail. He sends her a check so that she can give some money to Rod. At his brother's request, Rod is not supposed to know that his brother sends us his monthly stipend. Though she can't afford to pay anyone else, Sister has explained to Rod that she wants him to have the money because he does such a good job. And he does, too.

Unlike other volunteers, he's in the pantry every day. Though he doesn't actually work very hard, he is reliable. He has a bad attitude and causes people around him to feel uncomfortable simply because he's dirty and not much of a conversationalist. He collects cigarette butts to smoke at later times and says "shit" and "fuck" as often as he says "and" and "the." But once people know him, they adapt to him and his attitude. He even leads many of us to want to take care of him. You see, we are his family – the only one he's got. Without us, especially Sister Mary Ellen, he'd have little or no love and little or no contact with the world outside of himself.

Dorthea complained to me one time, "Father, the boy needs some better hygiene habits. It's kinda rough to be 'round him that way sometimes." She's right. I've only seen him wear the same flannel shirt and same pair of jeans, both in the summertime and in the winter. It's probably all he's got, or all he wants. We make sure he puts on different T-shirts though. Sister provides him with socks and underwear and we make up little care packages to present to him at holidays and on other occasions. On his birthday and at Christmas, Sister shops for him, usually outfitting him with a winter hat, gloves, a warm jacket or whatever she deems appropriate.

Rod's story is a sad one. He couldn't take care of his house after his mother died. He didn't pay bills. I guess he didn't know how. He was living there without heat or water; he didn't know how to cook or clean. The couple who lived next door, friends of his mother, tried to take care of him by checking on him every day, making extra food and sending it over. But they were quite old and there was only so much they could do to help.

That was when his brother contacted us and when Sister took Rodney under her wings. She definitely is a mother hen to him. Anyway, for good or for bad, he's been here ever since, but always in the background. He doesn't like to go around the clients. He likes to work in the pantry room or go on pick-ups and deliveries. He prefers to be alone.

Sister Mary Ellen has great respect for him and for her clients. She rarely gets upset. But one thing that can set her off is when parishioners or volunteers refer to them as "the poor" or "beggars" or anything else that hints at degradation. She spends ample time with each of her clients when they come for emergency assistance. She serves them as social worker, spiritual director, case manager, counselor and friend. She wants very much to empower each of them to become managers of their own lives. She has little tolerance for those who aren't actively seeking a better life and those who remain caught in destructive relationships.

She is continually making referrals: for G.E.D. programs, "Parents as Teachers" programs, cooking and nutrition classes, sessions on budgeting finances and stretching dollars, job training and interviewing, and anything else that seems appropriate. Whatever Sister and her clients, together, discern as the issues, she determines a path for them to travel where they can discover opportunities, or in some way expand their knowledge.

While she meets with the clients, the volunteers finish packing the boxes for them in the next room. They gather the frozen and refrigerated foods, as well as any vegetables, fruits or breads that we might have on hand, and add any literature we want to distribute to the neighborhood. Of course the fresh foods don't last long because by the time they are given to us, they're often no longer fresh. On this Thursday, the issue of refrigeration was not an issue, though. Sister and Dorthea prepared boxes for six households, but they suspected that not all would show up to claim them because of the inclement weather.

Saundra Mae Jenkins didn't respond to Dorthea's comment about somebody driving them home. But it was clear to Dorthea that she hoped it would turn out that way for the two of them. Ms. Jenkins did refuse the coffee but asked her hostess for a glass of water instead.

Sister Mary Ellen, who is in her sixties, was moving boxes around in the pantry room when the Jenkins' arrived for their appointment. Dorthea worries about the nun bending, climbing, and picking up heavy or bulky boxes. She compares Sister to me: always on the move. Though I am at least twenty-five years younger and move faster, Sr. Mary Ellen is much smarter and always manages to get a whole lot more accomplished in a day than I ever do.

Dorthea took the mother and daughter into the waiting room,

22

next to the pantry room. It contains predictable furniture from our establishment, most notably a long church bench. It is comfortable enough for those who don't mind feeling as if they are in church. And there are a couple of other old chairs from this, or some other, rectory.

On the walls are papers of various colors and sizes. On each of them is a thought-provoking quote, like "The one who wastes today lamenting yesterday will waste tomorrow lamenting today." Others read like this: "Parents who are afraid to put their foot down will raise children who step on their toes," or "The biggest room in the world is the room for improvement," or "We cannot prevent the birds of sorrow from flying over our heads, but we can refuse to let them build nests in our hair."

I overheard one of our volunteers say to another that he "don't understand what half of 'em mean, but if the priest wants 'em up there, who's to argue." Sister and I put them up – everything from Chinese proverbs to Christian beatitudes, in hope that they might inspire our clients and anyone else who visits our food pantry.

Admittedly, the signs were more my idea than Sister's. I had hung one that she coerced me to take down. It read: "Two of the most difficult careers are entrusted to amateurs: citizenship and parenthood." She told me that, even though she agrees with its intention, it might insult the clients.

I probably bombard her, and them, with too much paper and propaganda. She told me that the volunteers complained when I asked them to put papers inside the food boxes and bags. But I want them in there because I know that they will get into the homes of our neighbors and clients that way. The paper that they're inserting this month lists the "10 Traits of Healthy Families." The list includes important facets of family life like: they communicate, they share responsibilities, they teach right from wrong, they respect the privacy of the others in the family, they foster conversation at table time, and they seek help for problems. The volunteers concluded that there aren't too many healthy families among those who frequent our food pantry. I suppose they're right. Most of them probably don't ever have "table time" or privacy. Hell, some of them can't even read.

But I still maintain that motivational suggestions, like these, can potentially strengthen a few of these families. So I encourage it for those few. Sister was laughing when she told me of the volunteer's conversations and reactions to some of my requests. They said, "he's not quite connectin' with the folks he's tryin' to change, but we'll do what we're told."

When Ms. Jenkins and Reaundra sat down on the church bench, I came in from the cold looking for Sister Mary Ellen. Not knowing that she was in the pantry room, I entered into the waiting room that led to her little office.

I saw Dorthea first and made some joke about the cold weather. She said that it's reassuring at her age to see her own breath and that she's just glad to be alive. She is fun to joke around with, as are most of the volunteers. I made sure to thank her for being here on such a bitterly cold day.

Afterward, I spoke to Ms. Jenkins and her daughter. "Are you doing okay?" I smiled at them when I asked the question, but sensed that they could tell that I felt a little awkward. I didn't call them by name because I couldn't think of their names right at that moment. To them I suspect my question, "are you doing okay" sounded like I was valuing a friendship that we don't have. I wanted to say more, but I stopped myself when I noticed that all four eyes on the bench dropped down to the floor.

They said something like, "we's fine." But they were probably thinking something more like, "we's starvin' and freezin', and we just walked six and a half blocks fightin' the bitter wind while you was drivin' 'round in your heated up car." And they could have added, "and we's down here beggin' now 'cuz we can't pay our utility bill this month. And we left the children at home by themselves; and one of us is skippin' school, though none of us wants her to, most 'specially her, and our lives is pure hell since the boy is no longer with us." But that's not what they said. They just said something expected and something simple as Ms. Jenkins sipped from her third glass of water and passed it to her daughter. I left it at that. As I turned around to leave, the words of the 42nd Psalm flashed in my mind: "...my soul is thirsting for the living God..."

I'm sure that's what the volunteers meant when they said that I'm not connecting. It's not that I'm stupid, just ignorant. I'm ignorant of the ways of the people I'm supposed to be serving.

Also, I'm not sure why so many blacks seem to look down when I speak to them. I've been told it goes back to slave days. I've been told that black women are taught to not look at white men. I've been told lots of things by lots of people.

Growing up, I was taught that to look away is rude or unsociable. Perhaps my self-conscious feelings now merely symbolize my concern for being a minority. I sense the whispers of those who wish that their priest was black. But I'm just another one in a long list of white priests sent to black neighborhoods who thinks that he's trying to help, but who doesn't really understand.

Like many before me, I do try...to help and to understand. But I felt helpless standing over Ms. Jenkins. And I know that she wanted to respond to me, too. But something kept her from doing so. Maybe it's some kind of racial gap.

Simons Says

3

Dorthea told me that she tried to describe me to somebody and couldn't come up with anything to say except that "he's a average-lookin' white guy. He's of average height, not quite six feet tall, of average weight, between one sixty and one seventy, with average hair – not long, not short, the average color – brown, with average eyes of the same color to match."

Then she went on to tell me that I have average abilities, and that although I am of an average age for the general world (not yet forty), it is pretty young compared to most of the other priests she's seen.

"Most of 'em shuffle when they walk and slobber when they talk. They's even older'n me, Father. And some say they think I'm older'n God."

She seemed to enjoy describing me to me. "You're smart, but not so smart that I can't outsmart you. You look nice, but not too nice. You don't wear no fancy clothes or get so expensive with your tastes. You don't seem to like those gold chains or

26

rings or watches that some of 'em wear. You enjoy your friends and your family and your church family, and your work, too, but you don't enjoy none of 'em too much. You're just average. There ain't no other way to say it."

In one of our Thursday conversations, Dorthea said, "All you priests got your own ways of doin' things. For 'xample, you don't wear your black outfit that priests is known to wear. Oh, you'll wear it on the day of a funeral, maybe, or a weddin', or somethin' where it calls for dressin' up. But you don't wear it 'round your rectory very much, like some of 'em. I think that's okay, you understand, but some of your parishioners think it's a shame though."

"Why do they think it's a shame?" I asked.

"They say things like, 'he doesn't want people to know he's a priest,' and 'he's embarrassed of the church,' and 'he thinks it puts barriers b'tween his opportunities.'"

I suppose that by "opportunities" they mean that it is hard enough for me to connect with them already that I don't need an additional separation, like clerical garb, to make the chasm any greater.

She continued with her report. "One of your own Parish Council leaders says, 'oh, he's just tryin' to be one of us.' But I tole him, 'maybe Father just don't have too many of them black shirts. What does it matter anyway what he wears? Sister Mary Ellen don't wear her nun's clothes neither. But that don't seem to bother nobody too much.'"

"Do you think it really bothers them, Dorthea?"

"Naw. We all remember Fr. Alvin that used to do the pastorin' here. He'd put on that one thing – what do you call that fake shirt that's really just the front of a shirt, fits kind of like a tuxedo?"

"We call it a 'rabat'."

"Yeah. He'd pack that thing 'round with him and then put it on if he was gonna do priest stuff. Like Superman, he'd whip it out to visit the sick members at their houses, and then he'd take it off again just as soon as the visitin' was done. He always put it on if he had business down where the bishop worked."

I smiled. "You never know who you might bump into down there," I thought.

"And he'd always suddenly jump into it if he wanted a parkin' space at the hospital. But I wouldn't put that one past you neither, Fr. Thomas."

She said my name as though I should confess all my sins of taking advantage of our system.

I appreciate hearing her perspective on our church and the personalities involved in guiding it onward.

"Are there any other ways about me that you'd like to express?"

Her responses always seem to come quickly. I don't know if it is due to her sacrificing time to think, or if she truly does always have an answer.

"Well, you read a lot. And you're always encouragin' others to give their opinions 'bout the stuff we read. I don't remember another priest doin' that, here. And all those motivational sayins', like the ones you got hung up in the pantry, and all over your office upstairs – that's distinct. I noticed you even put them sayins' into the bulletins that get passed out to the churchgoers ever' Sunday. If you're askin' me, you overdo it a little."

I can always count on Dorthea for honesty. Not always for sensitivity, but always honesty.

"One other thing I wanna compliment you on," she added. "You're a spiritual man, for sure. Even if it is in a odd sort of way. Like you talk 'bout the Holy Ghost like it was a real ghost that walked 'round b'side you, kind of like some kids talk 'bout their imaginary friends."

After departing the Jenkins' and touching base with Sister Mary Ellen, I ran upstairs to accomplish a few tasks before my next appointment. In between appointments and meetings, I usually return phone calls or check in with a staff member or volunteer to find out how things are going. But on this day, I wouldn't get much done in between encounters. I intended to make some calls regarding a family situation that I had been dealing with for several hours earlier in the morning, but instead I opened a scriptural book to begin my preparations for the weekend Masses, only two days away.

When I did, I caught sight of the only pictures in the otherwise academic book. They are four pictures actually, tiny ones in the corner of each page that introduces a new scriptural theme. The pictures are of an ox, an eagle, a lion or a human. My eyes focused on the lion. As I paused from thinking, kind of like when I stood still from running around, it occurred to me that, most of the time, I either look behind to what has been, or I look ahead to what will be. Rarely do I look right in front of myself, to what is before me. And though I might be better off looking ahead now (Lent is only a few weeks away), my mind went backward to Advent.

I like the idea that the Gospel writer, Mark, is depicted as a lion. Mark's Advent story introduces Jesus' mission, teachings, passion, death and resurrection from out in the wilderness, where John the Baptist "roared out" to prepare a way for Jesus. It is as simple and profound as trying to wake people up – that is, wake up their faith.

But the Season ends with an Advent story from a different Gospel that focuses upon a different person who also prepared his way: Mary.

The topic of Mary is a divisive one in certain ecumenical circles. I realize that Catholic and non-Catholic churches hold differing viewpoints on the virgin birth. When I consider those who attend Masses at St. Peter Claver Church, there are Catholics and non-Catholics, as well as the majority of our members who used to be non-Catholics but who, for some reason or other, converted. It would be problematic for me to preach about her being conceived without original sin or her giving birth without intercourse. It is problematic because it puts her on a level that confuses so many of the "faithful." But unlike many other priests I have encountered, I don't mind problematic, controversial, or even dangerous territories, and I actually like preaching on the topics that might "wake people up."

Still, I am a Catholic official preaching tenets of the Catholic faith in a Catholic church. I try to keep historical data in its place and truth in its place, thereby encouraging listeners to grapple with their faith. Religion is merely a vehicle that brings us to faith.

What I find bizarre, though, are the many loyal Catholics who want to hear priests preach about Mary to reinforce their own religious image of her blue veil, her white dress, and the clouds underneath her feet. They want to hear good, sweet and kind pieties, niceties about her quiet virtues and how she treasured all those things in her heart. I avoid emphasizing that particular image because I think it reduces Mary's profound role of being the bearer of the enfleshed God, a role of great strength.

"Didn't they read her Magnificat?" I wondered. "Don't they understand her call for radical change? Don't they understand the social, economic and political reform that she announced that her God, our God, would bring forth for us? Can't they hear HER roar about preparing a way for the Lord?" That is what I was thinking as I stared at the lion.

While I was riled up already, my thoughts drifted back to a Sunday, several years earlier, when I was still living and working at Mary Immaculate Church, my first assignment as a priest. A well-dressed woman complained to me after a Mass, "I don't think God appreciates you saying the word 'screw,' and I don't either." She was furious, and barely getting started. "Don't desecrate this holy place of his. What would Monsignor think? You ought to be ashamed of yourself for talking like that."

30

One of the Scriptural Readings that day had been from *Jeremiah*, in which the prophet-author seemed madder than hell with the Almighty, protesting his vocation: "You duped me O Lord, and I allowed myself to be duped." In explaining what "duped" meant, I told the congregation that it "was a soft translation for what Jeremiah was really saying to God. Jeremiah was livid! He felt like he had been screwed over by God who was letting him know what real despair in this life was all about."

Perhaps my word choice was inappropriate for my audience. I admit that I do inappropriate things sometimes, even project my own feelings onto biblical characters to make a point. But I think those characters represent us anyway, both as individuals and as communities.

I hear foul language constantly around here – not only in the streets, but even in casual conversation with parishioners, clients and neighbors. Jeremiah's words were much cleaner than D.L.'s, or any other kid who tells everyone, and no one in particular, that he has been "fucked over by God." Is this discrepancy another chasm that keeps communities like the two I have served so far apart from each other? Do the two speak a different language?

I think Jeremiah was so angry because he had trusted totally in God, and he thought that God betrayed him. Talk about bad luck. Jeremiah had it from start to finish. I'm sure he didn't want to be a prophet. That was God's vocation for him, not his own choice. He probably didn't even want anything to do with God. But it seems that those are often the ones who God goes after. I suspect that Jeremiah carried out his religious vocation simply because God kept bugging him to speak to the people on his behalf. Like others before him and others after him, he decided to trust the Lord and he became a man of God. But he had a miserable time doing it. So naturally, he blamed God, the one who he thought "screwed him over."

One of the attitudes that can upset me is when religious people think that the Bible is supposed to be merely nice words and happy thoughts, and that priests and preachers are supposed to preach what sounds good to their ears. The Bible has some rather tough and painful messages to deliver to us. I don't think that they're supposed to be easy to hear. It's like the great author, Dostoevsky, once wrote about how love is much more than romance and infatuation and oceans of warm feelings. It is a harsh and dreadful reality, even tragic. It's a struggle that sometimes causes lots of suffering. God suffers a lot of painful love throughout the Bible stories. And if more Christians would spend some time reading them, they'd discover that they are not all nice and easy words that get communicated in the pages of that holy book.

And I think that that's the kind of life that Mary had to deal with, a life of painful love. It must have been very difficult for her, too.

I admire and adore Mary's role in salvation history. I look to her for guidance in trying to bring Christ into my world. I trust that she will help me discover him in this world of January's letdowns, after all the holiday presents have been opened (most of them already destroyed), after the lights have been packed away for another year, and after the desire for snowfall has long since passed. It is a world of high utility bills, a society of lingering hunger, and a neighborhood of apathetic citizens. I call upon Mary as my primary role model for discipleship. She knows what it is to find the Lord and follow him.

And since the greatest priest I have ever known, Monsignor O'Hara, departed from this world, I have called upon her as my chief example in priesthood, too. Unfortunately, I cannot find a whole lot of guidance from the priests who are still around. That is as much my fault as theirs. In one sense, on the day I was ordained I became a member of a brotherhood, but in another sense it is a brotherhood of loners. To make one of them a friend or spiritual guide takes more effort and time than I'm willing to expend. So, the Blessed Mother has, in recent years, become very real for me. She gives me strength and teaches me perseverance in facing the poverty and hopelessness that surround me at this church and which we encounter every day.

If it were up to me, I'd let us remain in Advent all year long. After all, we are always in a state of waiting, always in a state of hope. Dorthea, my chief advisor of choice, told me once that I am always talking about the Incarnation.

"You're obsessed with it, like it's too much to b'lieve, or like you don't quite grasp what the Bible's tellin' us 'bout God becomin' a human like us." She said that I tell too many stories about it, just hoping to convince others, and added, "but it seems like you really just need to convince yourself."

She mentioned one story that I told about a little Mexican boy who was dirt-poor. He didn't have any toys. But while playing by a trash dumpster in an alley one day, he came across a small aquarium. He took it home, cleaned it up, decorated it, and built a tunnel out of a tin can that he polished till it shined. He made a road out of marbles and got it looking very pretty. Then his mother let him have a quarter that she had been saving for food. For when she saw how excited her son was, she realized that she would have to give it to him so that he could buy a goldfish.

He was so happy because the goldfish was beautiful and wonderful. But after watching it swim for a while, he could tell that it wasn't enjoying all that he had done for it. It wasn't admiring the stuff he had worked on and created out of love. It didn't swim through the tunnel for him; instead, it went around it. It didn't notice all the shiny marbles and the other beautiful scenery. The boy yelled at his fish to try to make it see all that it was missing. In the end, though, the poor little boy realized that the only way he could show the fish how to understand everything would be if he, himself, became the fish.

"That's not the only one," Dorthea reminded me. "There's the one 'bout those barn swallows that wanted to get in the barn to get warm on Christmas Eve b'cuz they was freezin'. And the farmer wanted to show 'em the way, but bein' human, he couldn't speak their language. It would only work if he was one of 'em. It's the same kind of story, just with different animals."

She was right, of course.

"And don't forget the one 'bout the chile who b'came a dog," she continued. "That chile-turned-dog was so humiliated by his situation b'cuz it had already been a human and knew a higher form of livin'. But he had to communicate with the other dogs, and show 'em how to act, so they could appreciate what they had, so they could enjoy their situation as dogs more."

Dorthea was finally getting to her point.

"Father, it's almost like you want us to know that you had a higher form of existence b'fore you came to live in these ghetto parts of town, and like you wanna show us ghetto people that we can have a better existence, too – one that we can all enjoy and appreciate and that will bring us better understandin'. You're just upset 'cuz you can't b'come one like us."

She hesitated before making her definitive point.

"Sometimes when you talk to us, it's like you're that poor little Mexican boy that wanted to b'come the goldfish."

But I can't become who and what I am not, so I am compelled to roar out to get some kind of reaction or attention. Any kind.

When the doorbell rang upstairs, the doorbell to the rectory, my mind was still a month behind me, but my eyes stared at the lion before me. Jolted out of my Advent mindset, still waiting for a Messiah, I remembered that I was to meet with Mr. Simons, a neighborhood activist. He is one of those rare guys who have some hope to share.

Hope seems to be such a rare commodity in our area that I appreciate being in the presence of somebody else's hope. No, I ache for it. It is so difficult to stand alone.

I made it to the door quickly. We don't have a parish secre-

34

tary at St. Peter Claver. Nor do we have an associate pastor nor a pastoral associate nor a housekeeper nor anyone else to respond to the telephones ringing and doorbells dinging. As it is with many poorer parishes, volunteers like Dorthea and Rodney accomplish most of the work in our church. On days like this particular one, though, we don't encourage our volunteers to come to work. Those two just happen to be unique. When I encountered her downstairs earlier, Dorthea informed me that she had to be present today because she was certain that somebody would need her.

Mr. Simons is rather special, too. He fought the cold because, as he put it, "he wanted to be encouragin' to the young pastor that shouldn't be thinkin' 'bout what I know he's thinkin' 'bout. He shouldn't be thinkin' 'bout givin' up tryin' to lead this Catholic Church that got left in the inner city. This is the battlefield and a pastor is the general."

Mr. Simons brought one dominant theme to our conversations: "Your church needs to be concerned for the neighborhood 'round it. Yep, we're on the battlefield for the Lord."

This old man, my friend, helps me to realize that being a leader means different things to different people in our community. For a young, white man in an established, black community, to lead often means to follow. But in following, I can simultaneously guide. Just by walking down streets with some of my parishioners in search of clues that might help us find an abducted child or just by sitting alongside neighborhood activists across from a notorious drug house in protest, people recognize my leadership among them.

I've learned that a minister holds an honored place among many African-Americans. White or black, old or young, Protestant or Catholic, it doesn't matter. Mr. Simons, though not Catholic, respects my role and urges me to use my position to strengthen the neighborhood and to empower the residents who are "godfearin' and hopeful." That's what I want, too.

35

I trust that Mr. Simons will help me to discover my way. Though he is quite respected in the neighborhood around our church, he doesn't seem to ever accomplish much. He is a fine man, a gentleman, but like so many residents – even resident activists – he doesn't have what it takes to effect substantial changes. But he continually offers me inspiration and encouragement that gives me perseverance. He often tells me to not give up.

"Father Thomas, you know any dead fish can float downstream, but it takes a live one to swim upstream. You gotta go 'gainst the current sometimes and lead these people or they're gonna give up if they see you givin' up. God wants you to be alive to shepherd your flock that he entrusted you with."

After entering the rectory, Mr. Simons accepted a cup of hot coffee and sunk down into a chair opposite me without being asked. I am glad that he feels at home in our church buildings. I also poured myself a cup of the hot liquid hoping that it would motivate my mind for our discussion and somehow motivate my heart to care about another worthy cause.

Simons serves on our neighborhood association board and I serve on some urban development committees. So we first updated one another on the recent happenings within our respective neighborhood groups, and shared the plans and rumors that we'd heard since the last time we spoke.

Simons then made his never-changing plea.

"I've lived in this neighborhood for over thirty-five years and I've spent most of them years tryin' to make it better. I've watched a lotta my neighbors and friends move out. I've listened to 'em say they'd had enough, that they was tired of gettin' robbed. Ever' time one of 'em left, it made me wanna stay even more. But it's gotten to be the worst I can recall. We gotta do somethin'."

What muttered from my mouth spoke to a more global issue of which he really didn't care.

"I can't believe there is a violent crime committed in our na-

36

tion every five minutes. I suppose it's gotten worse everywhere."

I sincerely cannot believe it. It's one of those things that I simply cannot capture, that my mind cannot comprehend, that my soul cannot conceptualize; I can't accept that this is the kind of world in which I live.

I have trouble with other statistics, too. Like the number of people who are living on the earth – it is simply more than I can fathom. I keep thinking about how the world reached it's first billion citizens just over a hundred years ago, and how that billion has doubled in such a relatively brief time, then tripled, then quadrupled. Now there are some six billion of us. Soon, in the next century, we will be ten billion. All I can think is that we weren't able to take care of each other a hundred years ago, even a thousand years ago, and we can't seem to take care of each other now. With more and more of us, it will get tougher and tougher to manage the care.

But what really bothers me is that the more people there are, the more isolated all of the people seem to be. I have come to understand that loneliness has nothing to do with the number of people in our lives; it has to do with the kind of people that our hearts are willing to receive.

It often happens that after we get to the facts, we can get beyond them to discover the truth. Data about scripture and church dogma seems to me not unlike data about inner city life. Once we grasp the reality of the facts, we can begin to grasp the reality of the truth – a deeper reality. Many people, though, refuse to look at the deeper reality.

"I hope we can help alleviate some of the pain," I finally added.

Like Simons, I hope that our St. Peter Claver Church can make a difference. I am saddened that it hasn't yet, at least not in ways that satisfy me. I probably expect too much.

Mr. Simons spoke again, "I think what we gotta do is stop talkin' 'bout the crime and the gangs and the drugs; we all know everything there is to know 'bout it already. Ever' week, somebody else I know of gets robbed. Ever' month, somebody else I know of gets shot. Ever' year, somebody else I know of gets killed. What we gotta do is be adults to these kids, give 'em some opportunities, provide 'em some programs they can get to, programs that're their own."

We are both familiar with the plentiful studies about at-risk youth. We know about the high percentage of black boys who drop out of high schools, the high percentage of young black men who dwell in prisons, the high percentage of black girls who are single mothers, the high percentage of young black women who are on welfare, the high percentage of black children who violently die. We both know that the number one cause of death among young African-Americans last year, and probably the year before that, was homicide. And we both know that the best way to reduce crime and violence, and the rest of these statistics, is through greater involvement by adults in programs that will benefit young people.

Simons added, "Trust in the Lord. There ain't no problem he can't solve."

Though my mind's first inclination was to calculate the multiple negatives used in his last statement, my heart instructed me that to enter such an exercise would be to miss his point. Anyway, as I suspected, he was simply quoting another hymn. He often quoted hymns in the course of ordinary conversation. I realized that it would be a serious error for me to worry about sentence structure rather than current urban reality.

And that, essentially, is how our meetings go. We just talk about our concerns, talk from our personal experiences.

We talked for over an hour and a half, interrupted only a few times by the upstairs phone. That is the phone in my office, the phone for Catholic church business. But we could hear the phone downstairs ringing non-stop. That is the phone in the food pantry, the phone for people in need. And people call it for any kind of assistance they think they might get.

We were also interrupted for an additional ten to fifteen minutes when I did, in fact, give the Jenkins ladies and their boxes a lift home. I appreciated being given a second chance to talk with them to let them know that I, like Sister Mary Ellen, do care for their welfare and their future.

To collect the ladies, I descended the stairs to the pantry. Simons was a few steps behind me. When we reached the bottom, we caught Dorthea saying some final words to Ms. Jenkins and assisting her little one, who wasn't very little anymore, bundle up as best she could. She told Ms. Jenkins the same thing that she tells many of our clients who will listen to her.

"Trust in God," she said, "and pray, 'cuz things is gonna work out alright." I have come to know that Dorthea believes what she says. I'm sure that that is why she volunteers at the church. She often quotes for me, chapter and verse, a scriptural passage that is very dear to her. It is the eighteenth verse of the eighth chapter of *The Epistle to the Romans*: "The sufferings of the present are as nothing compared with the glory to be revealed."

Anytime she can relay the word of God to someone like that, she does. So when she said her good-byes, she instructed: "Ms. Jenkins, you just keep rememberin' that God's glory is so far beyond the pain you gotta go through to see it."

Then the mother and daughter walked to my car with me, our hands filled with food, while the old man made himself at home downstairs with Dorthea and Sister as he did upstairs with me. He talked at them, unsure if they listened, telling some of his stories while sipping from his coffee mug. Or as Dorthea tells it, "he just came down tryin' to waste our time, too."

My conversation with the lady and her daughter was better the second time around. Yet, as you will later understand, it was still difficult.

As I drove back to the rectory, I thought of how I want to share in Mr. Simons' desire to provide some programs and opportunities for the young people and the financially poor people who reside near the church. But I need a few more details than he had developed. After I returned, our conversation got redirected. As Simons told me about his visionary "program for kids" I realized that it is really nothing more than what he does already: just hang out where they do and tell them to give back to society in some way. What he does is that which Dorthea calls "wastin' their time."

Though Simons has no clear plan, to me it seems sort of like Jesus' plan for the program I now know as "Christianity." The New Testament plan of Jesus, like that of Simons, also gives no clear details. When I read the Bible, I find myself wanting more descriptions, more specifics regarding the who, what, when, where and how of it all. I want a plan, a strategy.

To me, the order of Jesus' ministry didn't match up very well with the geography of his journey. Galilee and Judea aren't close to one another by foot, but Jesus certainly did seem to spend significant periods of time in both of them. I would have written the story as a clear journey from Nazareth to Jerusalem, with all the memorable encounters unfolding along the way. And if it didn't happen that way, I'd want to insert a map so that every reader could retrace the Lord's steps back and forth.

I also regret that there aren't any descriptions of what Jesus and his friends looked like. Was his skin black? It must have been rather dark based on his Jewish and Middle Eastern roots. What color were his eyes? Could they have been blue, as one of my parishioners announced to me, and then added that she "got it on good authority." Her authority was a newsletter about apparitions and miracles from a group that promoted the phenomenon of Medjugorje.

On my drive back, I wondered about all this. Was Jesus gaunt as I picture gurus to be? Was he muscular as I picture carpenters? Was Peter short as I picture sidekicks? Was the Beloved Disciple an adolescent as his long life suggests? Was Mary

Magdalene as physically attractive as she appears to be in my own mind? And what about the landscape? Is a desert just another desert? A mountain just another mountain? A city street just another city street?

Perhaps, I concluded, the stories of our lives are more like a circle than a straight line as they move from genesis to destination. Though I prefer the Gospel "of the lion," that author sure doesn't tell his readers any more details than we absolutely need to know in order to believe. But maybe the details of the story aren't really that important to the story after all. Mr. Simons spends most of his days just wandering the streets of the heart of our city talking to other people in the streets and hoping that his words make some positive impact. Maybe his way is a better, more scriptural way.

By the time I pulled back into the parking lot, the fog was lifting. Once in the rectory, we resumed our conversation. We talked about the great number of immigrants and the drug and alcohol addicts who are getting cut from receiving welfare assistance, or health benefits.

As Mr. Simons pointed out, "Sure, some of them addicts spend part, or all, of their checks on maintainin' their bad habits, but many of 'em depend on them checks to provide their shelter, to purchase nutritional food, to buy necessary medicines, and even to try and break their addictions. I, too, was once lost, but now I'm found. Like them, I was blind, but now I see."

The choices facing those most affected by the Welfare Reform Bill are not easy choices for members of the targeted group to make. I hoped, indeed, that God's grace would be there to amaze them and see them through upcoming storms.

The two of us agreed that the primary reason that more people need help this first month of the new year has little to do with welfare reform, and more to do with the decision of the Gas and Energy Company to raise the rates of consumers. The increase is too much for our people. Those who used to be able to keep up each month simply can't. Both Dorthea and Mr. Simons have personally attested to that.

We also talked about single parents trying to rear children under very difficult circumstances. We talked about our neighborhood census tract "boasting" the highest percentage of welfare recipients in the whole metropolitan area and the highest percentage of school-aged children in the whole school district. We talked about the fact that this same area doesn't have any schools or any places for adults to work, or many safe places for children to gather and play.

We even talked about the Nintendo video games that little children play, where they become action heroes who beat the hell out of each other. These children seem to be permanent fixtures in front of their television sets, even in homes where adults can't seem to provide food.

Is no one else concerned that our societal value systems are backward? Does no one else consider the psyches of these children, which absorb such violent entertainment? Yes, we talked on many topics.

And as usual, in the end, Simons left me with something to ponder.

"Father, you came here four years ago lookin' at this parta town all wrong. You're startin' to see it clearer now. When you first looked at us, all you seen was a ghetto. I'm tellin' you that I may live in the inner city, but I refuse to live in the ghetto. You're finally startin' to trade in your ole sight for some insight. That way you can see the truth, and distinguish it from what's just a image you conjured up in your mind. When you see the truth, you can start seein' the future.

Then you're gonna develop somma that perfect vision you want so bad. Your eye doctor won't understand it, and your flock will appreciate it. They know your white church is used to puttin' peoples to sleep. But you can wake up whites and blacks to what their vision ought to be, if you try.

Seein' today and seein' tomorrow can make you both near-sighted and far-sighted. Your eyes can see the glory of his comin'. You may just get yourself some perfect vision after all. And you'll be able to see that the sun that rises over those abandoned warehouses and factory buildins' to the east of you is ever' bit as beautiful as the sun risin' over the beaches of those Marietta Islands."

Mr. Simons proudly served our country in World War II and often speaks of the beauty that he saw during his travels, especially in the Marietta Islands. He hasn't ever left Kansas City since, and rarely does he even leave the neighborhood in which we both reside, the area where he spends so much of his time just walking around, admiring it, and enjoying it.

It strikes me as odd that I never hear Simons say anything about the atrocities of the war he witnessed, or the destruction it did to those beautiful beaches and the beautiful earth that the sun lights up each new morning. Nonetheless, to me it matters little what we speak about. It is more important that we speak. It is important to me to be connected, even if I don't always connect. And, of course, I want to be inspired by other people's hope.

In one of his pastoral letters (Salvifici Doloris), Pope John Paul quoted a particular biblical phrase which I re-read nearly every day: "We should rejoice in our sufferings, knowing that suffering produces endurance and endurance produces character, and character produces hope, and hope will not disappoint us..."

From my experience, suffering really does depend upon hope, much like sin depends upon forgiveness. Without hope, the suffering all around me would turn into despair and disgrace. I think about that often. Hope will not disappoint us.

"Thanks for the coffee," Simons said with a hearty smile. "I sure was thirsty today."

As the old man trudged back out into the cold, I quietly prayed that I could see the sunrise on my tomorrow through his hope-filled eyes.

Sister Mary Ellen's "Gift from God"

4

As it happens each year, January faded out and February faded in. As it also happens each year, the shortest month seemed like the longest. But then again, what seems like it will last forever is soon gone, too.

Over a hundred different clients from a hundred different houses come to receive emergency assistance from Sister Mary Ellen and her team of volunteers every month. She doesn't get upset or concerned that more and more citizens need help making it by. I would, if I had her job. But she goes right along doing whatever she can do to alleviate the hungers.

She gives the poor souls food for their bodies for the simple reason that that is what they need. Oh, she realizes that they need other commodities more than they need food – things like poetry and art and music. She believes in the conventional wisdom warning, "the only way out of poverty is through education." She spent most of her adult years as an educator and she truly believes in its power.

Before coming to work at our food pantry, she was a college professor who taught theology and sociology. "I figured that the world already had enough smart people, but it needed some more good people. So this is where I wanted to put my time and energy," she informed me soon after we began working together.

She spends much of her time now encouraging our clients to get better educated, about both practical and impractical matters. Most of her clients are single-female-heads-of-households. She'll send one to get a G.E.D. if she thinks it will help her. If another has the ability and the interest, she'll find her a way to take some college classes. Sometimes the objective is to get the client a better job; sometimes it is for her to gain a specific kind of knowledge. Sister sometimes encourages a client to take a class in the field of psychology or literature or history, just as quickly as she recommends a class on computers or financial matters. I suppose that she has concluded that making the client smarter will eventually make the client better. But she realizes that formal education is not always the answer. Some people, like Dorthea, possess another kind of wisdom that comes from experience.

Dorthea only made it to the fifth grade. But as she explained to Sister, "You probly know there's a lot more to education than schools can teach. I learned a lot in the school of life."

Like many social workers, distraught by the efforts of the 1960s until now, Sr. Mary Ellen guides people from a position of receiving handouts to a position of self-management and interdependence. She and Dorthea discussed it, while working together downstairs one day.

"Sister what do you mean 'xactly when you say we're not 'bout givin' people fish, we're 'bout givin' 'em fishin' poles?"

Sister Mary Ellen rejoices in Dorthea's questions and in her interest. "I mean that the job of churches is primarily to teach," Sister explained. "That's why I like to meet with each of our clients, even though there are several hundred of them, so we can discover, together, what their real need is, and then devise a plan to help them attain it."

"I guess you mean that food ain't their real need," Dorthea quipped.

"It's their apparent need, but I think there's usually a deeper need," Sister replied.

"But ninety-nine percent of 'em don't call us 'cuz they want fishin' poles. They call 'cuz they need a fish for their meal the same day they's callin'."

"You're right, Dorthea. And that's why we give food for their emergency situations. And we also need to give each client a strategy or plan so that they don't find themselves in emergencies as often down the road."

"Sister, I guess we created our own mess that we're in today, don't you think?"

"In these past years and decades, people have learned the system we created for them very well. Some have learned only to be dependent on it and on others. It's not a very good lesson for us to teach our children."

"Yeah, I guess two or three generations of being dependent is plenty." Dorthea asked her next question: "How do you think we can go 'bout changin' things?"

"I think we've got to go slowly. The lesson we've got to teach is the lesson of love, and that takes time."

Dorthea wasn't through yet. "Sister why'd you wanna work in a food pantry anyway, and help people that didn't wanna help themself?"

Sister Mary Ellen thought about it for a moment before answering. "Jesus told his disciples to 'do this in memory of me,' and he wasn't talking about going to church on Sundays. He was talking about helping other people."

"How'd you figure to know what he meant by those words?"

"All I know is that after he said it, he got down on his knees and started doing something nice for them. He began washing their dirty feet – feet that had been traveling some long, dusty, and rocky roads. You can imagine what they looked and felt like. Dorthea, I think that Jesus taught us how to serve by his actions. I serve because I know that's the rent I've got to pay for living in this world with him."

"What do you mean? He's gone from this world now. He's already done his thing. We aren't livin' with him."

The nun responded, "I think we are."

After a quiet moment for Dorthea to think about the Jesus who visits them every day in the pantry, Sister Mary Ellen continued. "The way I read the story of Jesus, he just told us, directly, to do three things. First, baptize. Second, remember him – that is, make him real, make him current, in the bread and wine which some of us believe is his body and blood. And third, wash feet. I think that the church is real good at the first two, but I think we've failed at the third command. So I'm just trying to help out in that department."

"That's right, Sister. You said it right." Dorthea likes her friend, the nun, for she is a great example to her and to the other pantry workers. In classic Dorthea-style, she let Sister know of her admiration.

"I sure do like you, Sister. It helps that you're black. It helps even more that you're so dignified."

Sister did not get embarrassed easily, but Dorthea's compliment touched her and it showed in her facial reaction. "Thank you, Dorthea," she acknowledged softly.

Sister Mary Ellen grew up in the South, in rural Louisiana. She developed a strong work ethic early in her life, and it remains with her. There is something about her hands, her face and her eyes that those who encounter her can tell that she works hard and that she is sincere in what she says. She respects her clients at this stage of her life because she learned to respect all people from her very first stages. She treats each of her clients special; and they don't get much of that unique respect in their other encounters. Oh, she can be tough on them sometimes, but that, too, is a sign that she cares for them.

As director of the pantry, she determined early on that she could only feed one person at a time, and love one person at a time. So she takes her time and makes each one feel nourished with her compassion, as though that person is the only one for whom she needs to be concerned. She is the reason that Dorthea volunteers at our church at all. Dorthea first came to us as a client, herself, going through a difficult time many years ago. And that's why, even if she's the only volunteer on a particular Thursday, or if the weather is so bad that she has to put socks over her shoes and then put plastic bags over those socks just to go outside, she's going to do it. It's because Sister helped her once and she won't forget it. It's because the pantry remains open here for people like her, and that stable presence has become an important part of her life.

Sister Mary Ellen likes Dorthea, too. She likes all of her volunteer helpers. But there's a part of the nun that doesn't like or tolerate the actions of some people. I suppose that many of us who choose religious life do so because we were, or are, upset at the way things are, and mad at the people who we think make them that way or keep them that way. Many of us got into this work so that we could help change it, shift the wealth a little, and shift the power, too, while we are at it.

Saint Basil was probably mad at the rich and powerful when he told them that their extra loaf of bread belonged not to them but to the hungry. Then he went on to add that their extra coat belonged to the one without a coat, and that the money they stored up and left unused (their own) really belonged to the poor. However it was for Basil, Sister Mary Ellen has repeated his words to rich and poor alike. Though it's probably not a good way to win them over to her apostolate, it's reflective of who she is. She doesn't really care about winning anyone over, she cares about being a woman of integrity; she cares about doing her thing and paying her rent for living with Jesus. Besides, she's much tougher on the poor people who don't want to do anything to change from their current state of being than she is on the rich people who don't care to help.

But as the priest for this less fortunate community, I had better work on winning over those with money and compassion. I had better, simply because I'm the guy who is responsible for paying the bills and making sure that there's food in our food pantry to give away to those who truly need it. I don't agree with what Victor Hugo stated and Dr. King repeated, that "there was always more misery in the lower classes than there was humanity in the upper classes." Though the poor will always be with us, I'm certain that the only reason that St. Peter Claver Church is still operating is because of the generosity of wealthy people who have compassion for the less fortunate. Rich and poor have got to live together and work together on the same team so that we can battle the social forces of evil that attempt to defeat us.

Sister Mary Ellen and I make a pretty good team. We even have fun working together. And we respect one another. We also learn from each other, though I am clearly the primary recipient in that arena. Because I enjoy varieties of music, I am expanding her musical tastes. She told me that the music I lend her is broadening both her scope and her tolerance.

"Besides," she added, "I'm not too old to open my mind to a few new ways."

I have a sense of what she'll appreciate. As well as jazz, classical and country, I give her a lot of good old rock and roll – nothing that will blast her out of the convent, but sounds which she can understand and enjoy. I tried to loan some c.d.s and cassettes to Dorthea, but she wanted no part of my collection.

"Just let me keep my good Kansas City jazz, Charley Parker, Ella Fitzgerald, Cab Calloway...now that's some fine music."

The three of us agree that good music is what might actually unite different generations and different races, helping us to understand one another better and causing us to feel good about one another.

What I learn from Sister is primarily through her example. She teaches me about the struggles of black Americans and black Catholics. She finds books written by African-American authors for me to read. Dorthea got in on this exchange, too. She would take her Maya Angelou, but she wouldn't go for her Langston Hughes.

"Cusses way too much for me," she said.

Sister Mary Ellen also teaches me about prayer, different prayer forms, and how to discover God in other people and how to respect people for who they are, rather than wanting them to change into someone else who they've not been created to be. Not even intending it, she teaches me patience and acceptance. Yes, we do make a pretty good team, even if we might have gotten into this kind of work because we were angry.

Many of us who work with the downtrodden were probably angry once. Our anger is born of emotional reactions to the conditions of life and society – anything from war to poverty to institutional injustices. But we're trying to turn the anger into something positive by offering a hand to those who are victims, rather than just offering dirty scowls to those who victimize them.

At one of our neighborhood meetings, those in attendance learned that "anger" comes from a Norwegian word meaning grief. Of course, all good people should feel some grief for the disparity and barriers that exist between people; all good people should feel some grief for the opportunities that some children will never have; all good people should feel some grief for lives that travel down the wrong paths. It's okay to have the feelings that we have, which some of us protect and hold inside. And it's okay to get mad. Sometimes we should get madder than hell, because that's what it takes to bring about heaven. John the Baptist, out there in the desert, was probably mad – releasing his grief and allowing his anger to roar out so that people would wake up and do something worthwhile with the days with which God blessed them.

In this part of the city, I've discovered that there is a lot of grief and anger to be felt. It ought to be channeled into positive forces that will create an energy for which our children, and their children, will thank us. I think that we share in God's gift of creation by continuing to create what he started on the first seven days, thereby gifting others.

Rodney's Fate

5

People joke about Missouri's weather. It tends to be unpredictable from one day to the next. People say, "we're in Missouri," pronouncing the name of the State "misery." It may not be a state of misery that we are in, but it definitely is a state of confusion. At least that's the way it was in the months after I began this story.

The confusion has nothing to do with parents not knowing how to clothe their children when they send them outside. There is another kind of confusion in the air. It's as though people want something, but they don't quite understand what it is that they want, and they wouldn't quite know how to go after it, if they did know.

It has to do with Mr. Simons wanting to leave his mark on this part of town that means so much to him. It has to do with me wanting this church to have some special meaning to those who see it and who pass by it every day. It has to do with Sister Mary Ellen wanting her clients to get their poles and go fishing for a better life. It has to do with Ms. Jenkins wanting her children to enjoy the life she gave them. It has to do with Reaundra wanting to grow up happy. It has to do with each of us wanting these things, but at the same time accepting that these things we desire are beyond our abilities to capture. It has to do with hot and cold, just like Missouri weather.

The one among us having the roughest time is Dorthea. She wants something, too. But she doesn't know how to explain it. She is old and doesn't think she'll have much time remaining on earth. Her old age is a heavy cross for her to bear.

"Since it'll probly be the final cross I'll lug 'round, I wanna carry it right," she told me. "And I want God to let me know that he's right here with me when it gets to be too much."

She came to me recently longing for something deeper than she knows and deeper than I can give her.

"Father Thomas, I've been doin' me some talkin' to Jesus. I reminded him 'bout my good parts, and he reminded me I could do better. In some ways I know he's with me and wants me to come home with him some day, but in other ways I ain't quite sure he's with me. And I wanna be sure."

I tried to convince her that it is that way with each of us. Though I wished I could have offered greater assurance, I couldn't. That is part of our misery.

What brought all of this on for us, I suppose, is what happened to Rodney. During the cold days, the last of the dark days, Rodney complained to us that some of the people at his apartment building were giving him a hard time. Rod hadn't complained to us before. He cussed a little and complained about things in the world and in our society, but never about his personal life. It must have been more than teasing that he received from these perpetrators because it truly bothered him. They messed with his mind: kept him up at nights, hid in his room, took cigarettes from his table (he didn't have anything else to take), threatened him, warned him of imminent danger. They didn't talk to him directly, but from another room or outside his window. They talked loud enough so that he couldn't miss hearing what they said. He told one of the pantry volunteers that he was afraid that they were going to hurt him.

But he couldn't identify for us who "they" were. He thought that there were several of them, but he couldn't describe any. As I alluded to before, many young punks, drug addicts, pimps, hookers and gang members hang around his apartment, both inside and out.

One day Rodney didn't come to work. It was only the second or third time in all his years of helping out at the church's pantry. He didn't have a phone that we could call, but I know Sister was concerned about him. She claimed that she wasn't too worried, though, because he is a grown man and can take care of himself. But I knew that if he wasn't in the pantry the next day, she would be right down at his dangerous apartment building to find out what was wrong with him. As you might guess, that's exactly what she did. For certain, she found out what was wrong with him.

What was wrong with him was that he was dead.

One of the church members, a volunteer named Curtis, went to the apartment building with Sister Mary Ellen, saying the same thing that I had said to her before I went to my meeting: "If he doesn't show up, wait for me to get back. Don't go to his apartment by yourself," I cautioned her.

When they arrived, they knocked on his apartment door but there was no answer. A few hoods were hanging out on the front steps of the building, so after knocking for a while, she and Curtis started questioning them. But they said they didn't know Rodney. When Sister described him, they said that they hadn't seen him. There was no apartment owner or manager to be found on the site, so she came back to the church and called the apartment owner who lived in another part of town. The apartment owner said that Rodney died.

Just like that. He announced it to Sister after she asked him if he knew anything about her friend. Everything else, from then on, about Rodney's death was very strange. Sister Mary Ellen wanted some answers to her questions: When? How? Who found him? Why didn't anyone notify her? Where was his body taken? Was there a police report? The apartment owner wasn't giving out much information and wasn't very concerned about Sister's feelings. Furthermore, he didn't even seem to care that Rodney was dead.

Sister Mary Ellen, as you might imagine, was torn apart. She was Rodney's closest friend, yet it simply didn't matter to the apartment owner. She got mad because she had made sure that the apartment owner and manager had her name and phone number on file as the person to contact regarding Rodney in case of an emergency. But that hadn't meant very much to the apartment owner, either.

"Why didn't you call me?" she pleaded.

"I gave your number to the manager since he was the one that deals with the day to day business of the tenants," he said. "Two of us didn't need the number."

"But the manager didn't call me either!"

Two of them did need the number, as it turns out.

Her anger turned to hurt when she was informed that there is a different manager now. The apartment owner informed Sister that he wasn't coming all the way over to talk with her, and he couldn't let her into Rod's room anyway because she was not related to the deceased.

She knew she wasn't related. But she also knew that she was all that "the deceased" had. She was screaming part of the time and crying at other parts. Very frustrated, she finally hung up the phone after the owner told her that the manager wasn't around either.

When she put the receiver down, she got quiet for a very long minute. Curtis, who had remained with her, kept asking her questions. She responded to each one, but it was as if she didn't know what were the real answers. The input she was receiving that afternoon made absolutely no sense to her.

Rodney seemed to be down, emotionally, when he left work two days earlier, but that wasn't unusual. She wished that she had noticed something different about him.

It was late in the afternoon when she hung up the phone. Already it was dark outside. It was getting dark inside, too. The volunteers and clients had all left for the day by then, and no one else was around the church's rectory. I had not yet returned from my meeting. Sister just sat there, with her head in her hands. Several times she cried, though mostly to herself, that she couldn't believe it.

After a while, Curtis had the good sense to call another man who volunteers with Rodney too, and that man came to join them. Curtis also called the police station to inquire about the reporting of their friend's death. He was instructed to contact the city hospital to verify that his body was still in their morgue.

Sister knew that she would have to contact Rod's brother in France, but she wouldn't with so little information to tell. She decided that before she called him, she would return to the apartment, accompanied by the two men.

This time, they talked with everyone they encountered even though no one could, or would, give them any helpful information. The threesome kept asking questions anyway. They walked around the building, and located what they determined was his second floor window, barely opened. They even attempted to climb the wall, but gave up soon after they started because of their ages and because the window was clearly out of their reach. Finally, the three of them convinced another tenant to let them use his phone. They kept calling the office of the apartment owner until the manager finally did show himself. It was even darker by then, and colder, too. This was one of those cold days of misery. The manager finally opened the door to Rodney's room for them, though reluctantly. It was as if he enjoyed hearing them beg for each tiny step before he would permit them to take it.

Soon after that, I arrived at the scene, having returned to the rectory to find a note informing me what had happened and where they had gone. When I joined them, I was struck that the one room apartment was colder than the cold outside of it. And even though there was a light on, it seemed darker than the darkness outside, too. The window was opened up about four inches. The group said that it was open when they entered. There was no screen or storm window on the outside.

The manager was a strange character. He didn't know the answers to any of their "why" questions, like "why is the window open?" He jumped around a lot and didn't complete many of the sentences he began. He was shifty and kept looking around him. His eyes were bloodshot and he was constantly fidgeting. He said that someone had told him the day before yesterday, late at night, that the man who lived in this room was dead.

"Who told you that?" Sister asked him. She had switched to "who" questions at that point.

"The guy that tole me...tole me he was tole by some other guy...that guy said somebody oughta tell the manager...so I came here. Then I came here," he repeated. "He was dead...found him dead...laying on the bed...right there." He pointed to the right spot where the bed stood. "I called the owner...owner of the buildin'...owner tole us to call the police...we called the morgue at City Hospital and the police. That's what I done. They came and got 'em...got 'em right after that."

In the days that followed, the mystery of Rodney's passing from this world grew even more mysterious to me. It was a sad passing for many of us because the normal rituals of bidding farewell to both the living organism and the human shell were not made possible. It was also difficult because of the stories circu-

57

lating in the food pantry. Rod always locked his door when he was in his room. He had told several of us that much. But the door wasn't locked when the apartment manager "found" him. The police and the coroner's office released his body rather quickly, it seems to all of us. No investigation took place. No one was contacted, simply because those involved determined that there was no one to contact.

Our community gave him a decent Christian burial.

His brother from France said that he would come back to Kansas City for the funeral, but canceled his plans the next day after making them. He asked Sister to have Rodney buried very simply. He thanked her for the care that she, and our church community, had given to his brother. He promised to send some money, but couldn't until the next month.

I asked one of the funeral homes to donate the service. It was very generous to do so. But it wouldn't prepare the body, so the morticians just left it in a bag, and placed the bag containing the bodily remains inside the box.

No autopsy was performed. No cause of death was given. We were told that his brother was the only one who could demand those kinds of procedures. And he didn't. No one from the church even saw the body. I guess the official identification of him took place on the night that his body was discovered. Maybe Rodney's circumstance is just another case of bad luck. He was a poor, forgotten soul who had been overlooked by most people, the community, and the government.

His funeral service was nice, though. Lots of people from our church came. They came because, as Dorthea noted, "they remembered his family and remembered him as a good boy and they knew how loyal he was in helpin' the church durin' his last years." All of the volunteers from the pantry were there; they were his family. Nobody from his apartment building came.

On the ride from the church to the graveyard, I sat in the front seat of the hearse with the funeral director.

"What did this Rod guy look like?" he asked me.

I described him: "African-American, just over forty, about five foot ten and one sixty."

"That's not the guy we got in back of us. That's not the guy we were given to bury today," he said.

He didn't seem too alarmed by his own statement, as though burying the wrong guy happens regularly.

I was stunned. But why should I be? There are plenty of other poor, forgotten souls down at the morgue besides the one we came to know and love while he was still walking and breathing among us.

At the cemetery, while I was reading the prayers of Christian burial over the grave of whoever it was in the box suspended over the open pit, I stopped in the middle of one of the prayers because I saw something unusual.

Dorthea told me later that it looked like I had seen a ghost.

"You stared straight ahead for nearly a full minute."

The truth is, I did see a ghost. It was standing about fifty yards away, on the slope of the next hill, moving among the grave markers. There was a blanket of light snow covering the field, odd for late March. But the snow would disappear that same afternoon. The ghost would disappear in a moment, too, but only for a little while.

It wasn't the ghost of Rodney, though. It was a little man with white hair who had a big smile on his face, and who glided among the grave stones as though he was dancing. The man wore a green cap on his head and carried a black oak walking stick in one of his hands. His surroundings looked like winter, but the little man appeared, to me, like spring. He waved his free arm in my direction. Just then, I caught my composure and resumed the ritual prayers.

I didn't ever tell Sister Mary Ellen about my exchange with the funeral director on our ride to the graveyard. The whole situation upset me. I guess that those who get forgotten and mistreated in life are sometimes forgotten and mistreated after life ends for them, too.

Is Rodney's body still at the morgue? Nobody who knew him and cared for him even got to see his body to bid him farewell in the customary fashion. There is so much carelessness with human life. I wonder how our God receives him. However it happens that he crosses over from this world into God's world, I am certain that Rodney will be taken care of a whole lot better from now on.

The Devil Lucifer

6

There is a story told about a little boy who went on an errand. He took a very long time returning home, and his parents got quite worried. When he did finally arrive home, after it was dark, they started yelling at him. "Where have you been? You made us so worried!"

After letting them get their frustrations out, the child started talking. "When I was coming home, I saw my friend, the little boy down the street. He was sitting on the curb crying. His tricycle broke, so I stopped to help him."

His parents were still upset.

"Why?" they snapped. "How could you help him? You don't know anything about fixing a tricycle!"

The little boy looked up at them and answered, "I know that. I stopped to help him cry."

Sometimes it feels right to cry for yourself and sometimes there's nothing you can do but cry for others because there's just

61

no way to fix their situation.

Rodney's funeral was held during the week that we, Catholics, call "holy." Dorthea let me know that in her church, the Baptist Church, every week is holy. And for her, everyday that God lets us live is holy, too.

In our tradition, Holy Week is a time for us to consider the immensity of what God has done for us: his gift of love, his gift of life, the gift of himself, and his great passion. In contrast, it's also a time for us to consider what we have done for him: we have turned away from that love, taken away his life, we have rejected God, and have misunderstood his passion.

"The kind of thanks that God gets from us is real sorry," Dorthea says.

Holy Week leads up to Easter, and Easter is all about life and death and new life. God's and ours. Sister Mary Ellen speaks so powerfully of her love for this season. She says it reassures her that God will always triumph over evil and difficulties in ways that she cannot see or even comprehend. She said that even if she doesn't know what she is doing, it reminds her that God does.

"My job is not to know," she says. "My job is to trust."

I hold a little different viewpoint. My preaching during the Easter season reflects another faith. It is more like the faith and attitude of my dubious namesake who became known through the resurrection accounts in the Christian scriptures. In another life, that Apostle was probably from Missouri, too. In our "Show Me" state, we don't just accept something because somebody said it. We want real proof that we can see and even touch.

I suppose I'm looking for some real proof that God hasn't abandoned our inner cities the way that most of the businesses and industries and white residents have.

I suppose that I want some real evidence that God still cares about the poor people living around St. Peter Claver. He needs to care especially for the old people who are afraid to leave their houses, and the innocent people who are living next to drug dealers, and the young people who get tortured by gang members. I suppose that I want to see a sign which will convince me that Rodney will have a glorified existence from now on, along with his glorified mother who loved him on earth and with the glorified Lord who created them both. After all, wasn't God's intention to invite them to share in that glory forever?

My doubts are not a contradiction of my faith. They are probably important steps to my reaching a deeper faith. That's probably the way it is with many people. The apostle, Thomas, probably had to take several steps of doubt backward before he understood how much God loved him. Then he could move forward to claim Jesus as his Lord and his God. Even the apostle's doubt was a gift from above because it allowed him to take the next step as a step to belief.

Some of the people with whom I work in this parish joke that white folk think about faith way too much. They have observed that we measure it and evaluate it and renegotiate it with the Almighty, and that we shouldn't. They're probably right. If every time we pray to God about our faith and say things like "show me Lord, show me why I should believe you in this situation," or "show me how you remain with me through that situation," we're certainly going to be dwelling in the state of misery. Faith is not supposed to unfold that way.

Dorthea put it to me simplistically.

"Faith ain't s'pose to be somethin' you got to think 'bout. It's somethin' you just have. And then you thank God 'cuz you do. It's what gets you through those difficult times when there just ain't no fixin' the situation."

If the truth were known, I wasn't named after Saint Thomas at all, but rather for the Father of the Constitution, Thomas Jefferson. My father was a history buff and he named each of his sons after heroes of American democracy. My mom named my sisters, while dad named my brothers and me. But if it weren't for my mom, I would probably be stuck with a name like Jefferson Henry. She persuaded her young husband to go with Thomas Patrick instead, and then she told her own parents that my name honored the Patron of Ireland and that doubting apostle who found faith by seeing and touching the resurrected Lord.

Early in my priestly career, I looked for miracles that would strengthen my faith. Somewhere along my studies, I discovered that Thomas Jefferson had pasted together his own version of the Bible to read. It included all the Gospels, but deleted those stories in which Jesus performed miracles. I began to find value in that early president's belief system. I came to realize that miracles couldn't produce faith, but that my faith can produce some miracles. I don't much care for the kind of miracles that attract crowds and applause, though. Those kind of miracles didn't bring lasting faith to the crowds in Jesus' time, and they won't bring it in these days, either. To me, it is not unlike young kids who are looking for the miracle of crack cocaine. Sure, it will make them happy for a while. But it isn't real happiness, because it never lasts.

What I want is proof. Proof is something far more powerful than the miracles associated with stunts and magic and side shows. Proof brings lasting faith, something that miracles don't bring. Proof will not be found in magical signs, but in natural signs. Those kinds of natural signs have helped me to live through difficult situations, even when I couldn't fix them.

I mentioned to you previously that Ms. Saundra Mae Jenkins had an older son named Ronald. Her Ronald was killed last year, though, in a gang-related act of violence.

But, Ronald wasn't in a gang. He stayed away from them. He was a quiet boy, tall and handsome at seventeen. He was good to his mother, and he took care of the younger children in his family's house. He had a job at the Parkway Nursing Home cleaning, moving equipment, setting up the dining rooms and

64

performing other similar forms of manual labor. He went to school and to work, and that was mostly it. He wasn't much into sports or dating. IIe probably didn't have time, or maybe he wanted to concentrate on getting a good education first, like his mother urged him. Most of his friends from school lived in other parts of the city. Adrian and his crowd tried to pressure Ronald to join with them, but Ronald was real cool and he didn't give in to their pressure. For the most part, they respected his intentions and left him alone. But some of them were jealous.

One of the jealous ones was D.L.

Before I continue any further, I need to give you a little background on this crazy kid, D.L. I'll tell it to you as it has been told to me, many times by many people.

When his mother was a little girl, she was the oldest of several girls and one boy born to Mr. and Mrs. Johnson. They kept having children and they didn't know how to bring them up. Johnson was a drunk before they got married and he remains a drunk to this very day. He couldn't keep a job. He hasn't gone to work in over seven years. His wife was a disaster at rearing children. The babies cried all of the time, simply because they were hungry or thirsty or needed to be changed. She didn't realize that once a day was not enough times to change babies' diapers. It wasn't all her fault, though. She probably didn't have any clean diapers to put on the babies or any food to feed the children.

Whenever Johnson got a check, it didn't go toward providing for his family; it went toward providing for himself. Maybe he figured that if he was drunk, the crying would fade away. His wife finally left him and, as you know, she left the children behind, too. There was no divorce nor official good-bye. She just got up and left them all one day. It's been over fifteen years, maybe closer to twenty, and none of them have heard from her since her departure. She's never even seen her first grandchild,

65

D.L.

W.E.B. Dubois once stated, "American slavery gave the Negro three things – the habit of work, the English language, and the Christian religion. But there is one priceless thing that it debauched, destroyed, and took from him, and that is the organized home."

The Johnson home was certainly disorganized. On the outside it appeared debauched to the highest degree possible. And I suspect that its debauchery is due to some kind of slavery the inhabitants bring upon themselves.

Johnson's brother, Deek, was glad that the wife left because that meant that he could move in. Why he would want to, no one understands. But his own life must have been in total disarray for him to seek improvement by living with his brother and all of his brother's children.

The oldest daughter was about ten years old when her mother walked out on them. She was actually glad that her mother went. The woman was obviously not good in the enterprise of motherhood. She would beat her children to get them to stop crying. Of course that only made them cry more. When D.L.'s mother, that oldest daughter, was considered by her sober parent to be an adult, she was given the responsibility of caring for her younger siblings.

For that, she was unprepared. Though she may have wanted to operate differently than her own mother, the manners of parental conduct were already ingrained in her: hatred and neglect. The younger children resented their sister, and that was too much for her to handle, as it would be for any young girl her age. And her dad was no help to her because of his constant, liquored state.

But Uncle Deek came to the rescue. He helped her out, discovering how to get the kids enrolled in schools. It seems that no one had thought of that before. He gave her a hand around the house, cooking a meal now and then, and by simply being nice to her in general. The girl realized that no one had ever been nice to her before then, or helped her with any of her tasks before then. And she suddenly realized that no one had ever loved her before then.

Deek loved her in ways that she didn't need to be loved, though. He teased her and tickled her and chased her and kissed her. She was a victim of every adult who she had ever known, but he victimized her more than any of the others.

Nobody seems to know what the "D" in D.L. stands for, for sure, but Ms. Bodreaux determined that his mother named her child after the only person who was ever nice to her and who loved her.

She said to Saundra Mae, "He was named for his father who was also his great-uncle."

So, when she said, "thirteen's too young to be bringin' home a baby," there really was no "bringing" according to her own theory. The child was conceived right in their own house. But that was speculation on her part.

D.L. didn't know what his name stood for either. Adrian and his friends told him that it meant "damn-good look-out," referring to the early job that he held within their company. D.L. tells the younger kids in the neighborhood that it stood for "drug lord," intending to frighten the little ones and cause them to look up to him, adding, "ya betta watch out cuz the lord can destroy you."

To most people who live in our community, it just means another "dangerous leader" and another "deceptive liar" and another "demented louse" and anything else that reveals the underlying truth of his human condition. But to Saundra Mae Jenkins, it means that he is the "Devil Lucifer," himself.

You may wonder why D.L. isn't in school. I used to wonder about that, too. But I learned that the reason is as simple as the fact that his mother doesn't care and the fact that police officers have better things to do than take him there each day. If they had to spend their working hours dealing with truancy, they wouldn't have time for anything else. The sad part is that many of the

school-aged children want to be in school. But when they get
suspended from their school, they have to follow the district's
procedures for reentry, which begins with the first stage of waiting for the central office to contact them for a reinstatement hearing. That stage sometimes takes months.

The kids, however, don't wait around by the family telephone,
if their family even possesses a telephone. They go out where
the action is, where the other kids congregate, where phones are
plentiful, and so are guns, and drugs and peers in similar predica-
ments. D.L. is just another young person lost in that scenario.

Ronald got shot in a drive-by shooting. It was reported in the
papers as "a case of mistaken identity."

His body was detained at the funeral home for ten days while
Ms. Jenkins solicited money from people and institutions to give
her child a proper burial. For the funeral service, I was asked to
say something, even though I barely knew the Jenkins family.
They don't have a church or a minister of their own, and so, I
guess, they turn to St. Peter Claver whenever they need one.

During the eulogy, I quoted Charles Dickens: "When death
strikes down the innocent and young, for every fragile form from
which He lets the panting spirit free, a hundred virtues rise in
shapes of mercy, charity and love to walk the world and bless it."

I actually trust that something that good can come out of something that bad. His mother wanted to believe that it could, too.
But I don't think anybody else at the funeral service imagined
how it might happen.

D.L. didn't come by the funeral home. But he rode his bike
in front of the Jenkins' bereaving household a few days later and
yelled out for little Reaundra. But when Saundra Mae came to
the porch, instead of the girl, he flashed a grin, said "too bad
'bout Ronal," and then he laughed and rode away.

Maybe he was attempting to show compassion or maybe his
intention was purely malicious. I don't know. Ms. Jenkins chose
to think the latter.

The pain she felt at her son's dying was too much for her to take. Her pain lingers still. There is a gut-wrenching feeling burning inside of her. D.L. knows that feeling, and he knows just how to make it burn inside of the dead boy's mother so much deeper.

In the springtime, the people running our churches smell the fresh air and talk a lot about the Easter resurrection and Jesus getting us through our trials and tribulations, sort of like he got us through the winter. At the same time, the people running our neighborhoods smell the same fresh air and talk a lot about other things – things that don't necessarily bring out new life. The streets in our part of the city get filled with people most hours of most days in the spring. Everywhere I look some days, young children are playing. Teenage girls are taking off the layers of their clothes, and some of the boys are up to no good.

Note that I wrote "some" and not "most." Most of the young men are fine kids who are just having fun. But those in Adrian's company are not among those fine young men. On one particular Friday afternoon in early April, D.L. and his friends were hanging out on 27th Street in the front of his house, contemplating what kind of trouble they might create. I think their foundational problem is that they have way too much time on their hands and they are motivated by the wrong forms of entertainment.

But I sometimes think that most of us have too much time on our hands and we are motivated by the wrong forms of entertainment. For example, it used to be that on first Fridays, Catholics would flock to their churches for special services and special blessings. But since the gambling boats moved to our river town, and since first Fridays mean payday for many of the urban poor and since the church lost its draw, they now flock to the boats to try their luck. They can't wait for their reward in heaven; they want a more immediate reward on earth. But their luck usually comes up bad. Though the new habit causes grief to me and other church

69

leaders, it doesn't seem to hinder the devotion of the people to their new first Friday ritual.

Meanwhile, Sister Mary Ellen pursued her routine for first Fridays. She left the pantry at her regular time, four o'clock, to go home to the convent and prepare for her class that evening. The convent is a typical house. It is in a row of similar looking houses on Spartan Parkway, less than a block from our church. The parkway is well lit at night and the nuns feel safe living there. She and the three other religious women who live with her took the necessary time to acquaint themselves with their neighbors, and those neighbors are quite happy that there is a house occupied as a convent in their area. They figure that it blesses an otherwise cursed stretch of real estate.

Of the other Sisters, one is a teacher in the only Catholic elementary school that remains open in the central part of town, one works as a chaplain in a hospital, and one is a social worker in an agency which provides shelter and counsel to battered women. I suppose that they each have their hands full. The class, to which I just referred, is one that these four nuns dreamed up and now teach, right in their own domicile on the first and third Fridays of each month. The class was designed for young girls in the community – to teach them some practical household skills that would "help them help their parents in their homes."

That was how the Sisters presented it to the young women and their guardians, even though most of the girls had only one parent, and even though that parent saw little value in the skills that are being taught to them.

Its curriculum is a variation of home economics. Sister Raphael, who teaches seventh graders during the academic year, selects most of the girls from her school. Sister Mary Ellen and the nun from the battered women's shelter also recruit some students who they believe will benefit from these sessions. The nuns realize that ten, eleven and twelve year old girls are expected to do so much in their households for which they aren't properly prepared, so they teach girls some of the basics.

They teach them about cooking and baking, making sure that the children understand nutrition so that the little brothers, sisters, and cousins in their houses won't fill their stomachs with junk food most of the time. At each class the girls cook a meal and eat dinner with the four adult women. They always make a lot of extra food so that each child can take some leftovers home with her.

The Sisters also teach them how to do laundry. One of the girls gets to bring some of the laundry from her home with her, and the others help her sort it at the beginning of the session and fold the last load near the end. They teach the girls how to sew simple things, like a button or a hem, and once in a while one of the nuns will illustrate for them how to do needlepoint or how to crochet. At Sister Mary Ellen's urging they also read and write poetry or tell stories or play music. One time they even went to a musical play together.

The nuns believe that these young women have far too many pressures on them in their houses that get complicated by the additional pressures of being girls in a culture in which some males view them as objects more than as humans. Sister Raphael once told her housemates, "If a premature frost withers the flower, it might not ever open up and bud again."

Yes, too often, when a girl gets hurt at a young age, she never gets over it.

Sister Mary Ellen was glad that Reaundra Jenkins would be present on this particular Friday. The girl's mother liked the influence that her friend from the food pantry was having on her family. She also appreciated what the nuns were teaching, and that her daughter was being exposed to such nice women, even if neither mother nor daughter fully grasps the purpose of the religious women's peculiar lifestyle. The nun offered to pick the girl up at the Jenkins' rental home, but her mother declined the offer.

"Just bring her home if it's startin' to get dark; otherwise the exercise'll be good for her," she told the nuns.

Sister Mary Ellen was thinking about the two Jenkins ladies as she undressed and stepped into the bathtub, an especially soothing ritual after working hard all week long. She put in a cassette that I had loaned for her listening pleasure. It was by a group called 10,000 Maniacs. They were singing about the Garden of Eden.

"We are the roses in the garden, beauty with thorns among our leaves. To pick a rose you ask your hands to bleed. What is the reason for having roses when your blood is shed carelessly..."

The soft, melodic voice of Natalie Merchant had a calming effect on Sister Mary Ellen. She looked forward to a relaxing weekend and an opportunity to help water some of the budding roses of God's garden who would soon come to her house for a lesson and a meal. And Sister realized that what they would really get is a glimpse of a better world than the one in which they spent most of their time.

There was different music blaring down the street – gangster-rap, the stuff in which Sister (and Dorthea) can find no redeeming qualities. It seems to fit in with other things to which many of us don't relate. As Dorthea put it to me, "It makes no sense at all, boys in jeans saggin' down b'low their buttocks, 'ebonics' gibberish we can't understand with all of the pointin' in ever' which direction that goes along with it, and filthy language that none of us should tolerate from nobody's mouth."

The music from one of the parked cars was so loud that the vibrations were felt several blocks away.

Reaundra felt the vibrations, also, while still two and a half blocks away from D.L.'s house. Because she didn't want to walk into trouble and get harassed by the boys, she quickly darted for

72

the next corner and took a right so that she could walk down 28th Street. She would arrive at the convent a half block from the south, rather than the north.

D.L. would have never noticed her if it wasn't for the Caucasian driver steering his vehicle onto the boy's block. D.L. didn't like white folks, and he hated to miss an opportunity to insult or scare one.

"Get da hell outta my neighbahood, white pussy."

He yelled his demand forcefully, looking right into the driver's eyes as the car went by, and he ran into the street to emphasize his point. The driver was lucky that the partying hoods didn't block the street, as is often the case.

"Get back ta ya own god-damned sida town."

When the car continued on, the driver checked his rearview mirror to see D.L. standing in the middle of 27th Street, flipping him off with both hands held high in the springtime air, his can of beer stuck down the front of his pants. D.L. has piercing eyes, and I'm sure that the driver of the car will remember his young face. He is short for a teenager. His skin color is light, almost white, similar to his Uncle Deek's. And his eyes are a sparkling green color, unlike other family members except his grandmother Johnson who, we've been told, had very, very unusual eyes.

When he turned around in the street, D.L. caught sight of the young female on the sidewalk, carrying a bundle, and scurrying south onto Euclid Street. He was bored with his friends so he jumped onto his bicycle. He reminded the gang to watch for the police because it was about time for them to drive up 27th Street, making their daily trek over to the Avenue, where the dens of crime would keep them busy for the remainder of their shift.

The kid gulped down some more of his beer and threw the near empty can back toward his own residence, attempting to hit one of his buddies.

Sister Mary Ellen dried off from her bath and sat down to

pray. She would be saying her evening prayers with her religious Sisters after dinner later that night, as she does every night. But she finds comfort in her own personal prayer and silent time, which she tries to find each morning or afternoon. The prayers that she likes to offer at these times aren't the long-winded verbiage of other theologians who write for missalettes and prayer guides. Sometimes she'd simply read a passage from the Bible, spending these precious times meditating on a line or phrase that Jesus is presumed to have spoken. Or maybe she'd reflect upon the words of some other spiritual guru, or perhaps she'd forfeit the words of another in favor of silence which allowed her to think about one, or several, of her clients. She often found it helpful to her ministry to lift them up prayerfully to God for some special remembrance.

On that particular Friday afternoon, she had two meditations. The first was from Jean Vanier: *"Christ put into the arms of His church the suffering and the hungry of this world so that they may heal us, call us down from our pedestals of power and wealth, and lead us into the wisdom of the Beatitudes."*

The nun began to reflect upon the eight Beatitudes and consider what kind of attitude it would take for her to be more like Jesus. She considered the kind of power and wealth that she held onto in her life, and prayed that God would heal her and lead her to open up her arms to soothe and caress the suffering, and feed and nourish the hungry with the same attitude that he carried. She became lost in her meditation that eventually brought her thoughts back to the girls who would be arriving shortly.

D.L. turned onto 28th Street from Corinth, the perpendicular street at the west end of his block, and he saw Reaundra just a few yards away. The young girl tried to hide the fact that she was scared. She was mad at herself for going right instead of crossing over to the left, so that she could have walked along 26th Street. It was always busier with traffic and pedestrians. But the street on which she ended up looked to her like the only street of a ghost town.

"Whadaya 'fraid of, Reaundra?" He laughed as he spoke.

"I'm not," she retorted. But the way she said it informed D.L. that she was more afraid than she appeared.

"Where're ya takin' ya bed sheets? Plannin' ta sleep out, start earnin' some money as a ho?"

He turned his bike onto the sidewalk and began to peddle alongside of her, bumping her off the sidewalk and into the yard. "Don't be takin' afta' ya mama now."

"The sisters at the convent is expectin' me," Reaundra replied. She clutched her laundry closer to her body, while he began grabbing at the loose material. When she clutched it tighter, he started going after the blouse that she was wearing, instead.

"Leave me alone!" she screamed.

That was enough to make D.L. angry.

"Them sisters is nothin' but hos – teachin' ya own black ass ta be one, too."

Though he was fuming on the inside, his mouth revealed a conniving smile. She had seen that look on him before.

He continued his assault, "Everbody knows da Catholics fuck with ya mind. Da only reason dey gives ya any food is so's dey can get in ya pants. White bastards and bitches are tryin' ta take our neighbahood 'way from us. Ya's stupider'n ya look if ya's listenin' ta dem."

Reaundra decided to run. But D.L. anticipated her move and rammed her with the front wheel of his bike. It knocked her down onto the dirt and garbage that rested in front of a once boarded-up, and still abandoned house which had been posted with the familiar ordinance on its front entrance: "Trespassers Will Be Prosecuted."

Sister Mary Ellen had already switched to her second meditation, a prayer by Saint Teresa of Avila: *"Let nothing disturb you. Let nothing frighten you. All things are passing. God alone suffices."*

This prayer gave her courage. She hoped that it could help her bring courage to others, too.

As she thought about the kind of courage she needs to possess, she suddenly could hear the cassette from the next room again. Somehow she had blocked out the music all the time that she was praying. She was good at blocking one thing out when she focused on something else, like the way she blocked out the rap-music that was pounding out from down the street.

But the words of another song, "Tolerance," made their way to her ears now.

"The still and silence is torn with violence...the sound you're hearing, the sound you're fearing is the hate that parades up and down our streets, coming within bound and within reach."

The soft voice of the vocalist startled her, so beautiful and yet so strangely penetrating. It got to her in a painful kind of way.

Both sounds were now coming at her with incredible force, stronger and stronger. She went to her window to close it. When she did, she pushed it with all of her strength. She was frustrated because she couldn't force it to close completely. She could not shut out the violating noise.

Reaundra screamed again, but on that Friday afternoon in nearly seventy-degree warmth, no one had the ears to hear her voice. Most of the structures on that 28th Street block seemed abandoned and condemned. Her scream mixed with the piercing sounds of the gangster-rap that was shaking up the neighborhood on that glorious afternoon. Pieces of her laundry added to the trash that littered the street and sidewalk already.

D.L. hit her, commanding her to "shut up." When she tried to fight back, he hit her again, his fist landing right in the middle of her face. Then he wrapped her arms in her own bed sheet and carried her into the deserted house.

76

"Why'd you and ya goddamned muthafuckin' mama call my mutha a ho? Da Bodreaux bitch is crammin' ya heads with lies. She was thirteen – so what? In nine months you gonna be thirteen, too. You da ho, not my mutha!"

When he got her inside the dark dwelling, he ripped her blouse again and knocked her to the floor. She was trembling. Blood was gushing from her nose; her head hurt – she could feel a bruised spot above the back of her neck. She attempted to scream, but she couldn't any more. Nothing else would come out. She couldn't catch her breath.

"Oh mama, oh mama – help me." But the words wouldn't form.

D.L. was overtaken by his hatred. His eyes were on fire. Rage imprisoned him and evil burst from within him. He hit her again and again.

"Ya cunt-motha can't blame me for Ronal'. He was stupid."

She lay there, powerless even to breathe on her own. The boy stood over her, a shadow in the darkness. The pounding music vibrated from the block behind them, getting louder and louder. He unzipped his jeans as he knelt over her. He pushed away what remained from the small bundle of dirty laundry and got on top of her, moving the bloodstained sheet up from her chest to cover her face.

"I can't stand ta look at ya, bitch," he sneered.

As though half of her was buried alive and half of her was violently tortured, she was frozen and terrified, helpless to change her fate.

The song continued to tell its truth as Sister Mary Ellen exited her room to welcome the young girls for their class about practical skills that will help them out and make their lives a little easier and better and healthier.

"There's something seething in the air we're breathing. We learn slash and burn is the method to use. Set a flame...we're

77

overpowered. We kneel, we cower, we cover our heads. Feel the threat of blows that will come and the damage that will be done in its wake."

All Alone in Darkness

7

Kneeling in the darkened church all alone, I read the words from my breviary, *"O God, you are my God, for you I long. My soul is thirsting for you like a dry, weary land without water..."*

I tried to offer my prayers for those who truly needed them, for those souls that I was sent here to serve. But, like so often, I felt incapable of serving them. And worse, I was unable to admit it.

As you have probably gathered, this story I've been telling you isn't intended to be a story about nourishing stomachs through our food pantries, to rid them of their bodily hungers. It's about nourishing souls through our human contacts, to rid them of the spiritual hungers that plague us all. It's about knowing how the flowers felt.

All I could think about, as I tried to pray, were the multitudes of people who come to church to see Jesus. Jesus meets them. Jesus touches them. Jesus saves them. Then Jesus leaves them.

79

He goes off to some deserted place to commune with the Father. And the people get hungry once again. And they are all alone again.

The little Jenkins girl, raped and beat up and then left for dead, is a tragedy beyond restoration. Her mother had her heart ripped out and torn apart again. She would have traded places with Ronald without having to think about it. I know that she would. He had a future filled with possibilities. She longed to trade in her life for his. And I also know that she would have suffered in place of her daughter, and ten times the torture and humiliation if only her child could erase the suffering which she endured and continues to endure.

What's amazing to me is that Saundra Mae didn't hate the church that offered her hope and, at the same time, yanked it away. She didn't hate the nuns who summoned her child to them to learn the wrong things that children need for survival. She didn't even hate me who kept trying to convince our neighbors to trust in God by trusting in the church's ability to make it a safer neighborhood. And she didn't hate the God who claims to hear the cries of the poor, but who allows such horrific atrocities to happen within our reach, and yet beyond our grasp.

But she did hate D.L., and she hated the legal system that would pit his word against that of her baby's...her bruised, broken, battered, and bleeding baby. She hated that he would once again walk away from an act of evil, that he wouldn't have to pay enough for the crime he committed. He never had to pay enough. He was never forced to hurt – as he should, in justice, hurt. The way she hurt.

My search in the prayer I offered in the early hours of morning, and my search in the work I will offer in the days and years ahead, will not be a search for justice. Justice is not to be found. Mine is a search for God's love, which must exist somewhere in the injustices that rise up all around me.

It was not yet seven o'clock, and the dark chill of the spring morning whispered messages too soft to enter into my soul. I considered the Prophet Elijah, who waited in the cave on Mount Horeb – waited for God to come by him. As he waited, he could not find God in the earthquake or in the strong wind or in the mighty fire. But he discovered God, finally, in a tiny whispering sound – in the sound of silence.

I read the Psalm from my copy of *The Divine Office* again. *"O God...on you I muse through the night...my soul clings to you...hold me tight. As morning breaks I look to you to be my strength this day."*

The helpless condition I felt drained whatever energy I may have soaked in during my recent few hours of sleep. I realized that God, alone, could offer me new impulses for living out the day that lay ahead of me. As I walked out of the sacred building, I gazed up at the first hints of day breaking in the eastern sky. There were soft colors, pink and orange and a gorgeous deep blue. They were mixed up together, providing an ironic backdrop for a factory's tall smoke stack, a massive brick warehouse with busted glass for windows, reaching limbs of old trees with new buds, and rows of roofs covering rundown houses and apartment buildings.

This is where I live. I was struck by how beautiful the sunrise looked that morning.

BOOK 2

In Search of a Dream

"The modern man is more like a traveler who has forgotten the name of his destination and has to go back whence he came even to find out where he is going."

– G.K. Chesterton

From Baptism into Life

1

The immersion of an infant during the Baptismal ceremony at St. Peter Claver Church earlier in the day was uneventful for the tiny, naked child who got dunked three times. The baby's great-grandmother also seemed unaffected by it all. But for the parents, grandparents and others in between the infant of focus and the octogenarian, it was a celebration worthy of gasps, applause, smiles, tears, and lots and lots of pictures.

With everyone focused upon the child of grace, I am quite certain that no one heard the line from *The Holy Gospel According to Luke* that floated around in my own mind many hours later: "...When you have done all that has been commanded of you to do simply say, 'I am a worthless servant, I have done no more than was my duty'..."

The assembled people would much rather have heard the story of Jesus scolding the disciples from hindering the little ones, saying, "Let the children come to me...it is to them that the Kingdom of God belongs."

It may seem odd to ritualize a beginning from the vantage point of the end. But that is what I was thinking.

Ten hours later, I found myself in a hot tub in the backyard of my friends' house. As I slid my head underneath the surface of the warm water, it was easy to imagine the chaotic waters, bubbling up, at the very dawn of creation. In the beginning there was darkness and disorder – a formless wasteland from which life would emerge. I sensed life rising up from the primordial baptismal experience: buried underwater, separated from life as we know it, cut off from the five senses.

At that moment it seemed natural for me to acknowledge the dominant power of H_2O: within the womb, inside the body, upon the earth. It seemed right to consider its multiple forms: rain, ice, and steam, solid, liquid, and gas. Water impacted life and death throughout history: in the devastating flood of Noah's time, the parting of the Red Sea in Moses' day, John's ministry in the Jordan River, the blood and water that flowed from Jesus' side at the hour of his death.

As I resurfaced into the cool night air, caught the power of the strong wind, and looked up into the starlit sky – the kind of sky that is rarely visible from my own inner city domicile, I felt somewhat guilty leaving it simply because most of those among whom I have been sent to live, never can.

This sort of Sunday evening escape is not a routine for me, but is also not unusual. Friends from college, now married to each other, invited me out beyond the suburbs to their family table for dinner. Another couple, also friends from those former days, joined us. The large deck off the back of their spacious home led to a wooden gazebo which housed the hot tub in which I sat and soaked. The five of us came out for a dip in the water after the children of the house had gone to bed. The water is as nice in mid April's spring as it is in any other season.

The last time I found myself in this water was in early December at a previous gathering of our small dinner club. I enjoy get-aways like this one. Though I attempt to justify it in my own mind as being similar to Jesus escaping from the crowds and going off to another shore to find a deserted place in order to get refreshed, I know that the parallel isn't a good one. Yet I keep trying to convince myself that it is.

Even after my friends had gone back inside to dry off and return to their own routines in preparation for the work week ahead of them, I remained behind to finish my drink and to be consumed by the frothy waters that warmed me. As I took a sip of the whiskey in the glass, I contemplated why I thirsted. What was I thirsting for?

Alone again, I thought about the Spirit of God which mythically hovered over those waters of chaos so long ago. That holy presence brought order to the disorder of it all. From then till now, water is symbolic of birth and rebirth. It brings order to all disorder of life.

I guess that's how the process of creation moves: from disorder to order. Before departing the waters, I submerged myself again and resurrected into the cold, cruel world, breathing an air of renewed hope for the infant child whom I had held in my hands that morning. It even gave me hope for the baby's great-grand-mother, hope that a rising would succeed every dying.

Coming up out of the waters I opened my eyes, and through the steam rising around me, I saw the figure of an old man sitting on a patio chair across the deck. After squeezing my eyes closed again, and then reopening them and wiping them dry, the figure had vanished.

As I drove home in the night, I thought about the original mystery of life and the final mystery of the human soul. Somehow my life and the lives of my friends fit into that mystery. It is the same mystery into which the child got baptized: Father, Son and Holy Spirit – Creator, Redeemer and Sanctifier. We share in that triune mystery: mind, body and spirit – thought, word, and deed – id, ego, and superego – interior life, visible self, and invisible union. It is the mystery of our being in relationship with others, with ourselves, and with our God.

Once in a while, and usually at times like this, I become lonely and crave the intimacy of the married state that my friends know. Getting through the night is sometimes difficult.

I long to embrace as a loving, protective, husband embraces his wife. During dinner my friends had swapped stories about their children, and more stories about their parenting, which caused me to yearn for another intimacy. How precious the manifestation of love for another person in the embodied flesh and blood of their own creation must be, totally dependent upon its creators for learning about life, and for life, itself. As love spreads though, I suppose it must eventually become too much for any man to embrace.

As a celibate priest, I, too, am called to love. Certainly a celibate priesthood without love defeats its own purpose. At the risk of seeming corny, I think I have somehow been given the grace to remain loyal to my celibate commitment, but at the same time, the grace not to forfeit loving. I don't intend to regret anything significant about my vocational choice. For I have made a good choice.

Life is a series of choices. Something is gained and something is given up in every choice that gets made. I know that I can live with this choice I made. But will I live it lovingly? Can I live it joyously?

Going through my imagination were extreme ways in which various types of people might be spending that very night. Basil the Great (a fourth century Turkish saint who wrote numerous documents and letters of which over 350 have survived) did not think that the night of a man of God should be spent only on sleep, for then that man might render useless half of his life. But

Basil's instruction wouldn't be popular in our modern society that bore the task of bringing closure to the second Christian millennium. Nor would he get called "great" in the here and now, for he proclaimed that the night should be divided between sleep and prayer. "How many 'men of God' would be doing that this night?" I wondered.

When I arrived home and got into bed, I was very relaxed, very tired. And yet, at the same time, I was restless.

The Dream

2

It was so dark when I slipped out of my bed in the middle of the night. I didn't want to make any noise or turn on any lights, afraid that I might give away my position to the imagined robbers who woke me. I moved secretly down the stairs to a place near the front door and crouched down under a window. I saw shadows scurrying along the outside of the house. From my place of hiding, I tried to peek out of the glass to see what I could see. Then, without warning, the doorbell rang. I saw a big, mysterious-looking man in dark clothes; he was wearing a hat with a wide brim and an oversized overcoat. The man called through the door that he was with the U.P.S. and he needed me, the resident, to sign for the delivery he was making. Without much reluctance, I opened the door to receive the delivery, and the big, mysterious man pushed his way through the front door, overpowering me. Several others were in back of the big man, breaking loose from behind his huge coat and scattering in all directions to overtake the house. Most of them were little children. They

*looked unkempt, dirty and scuzzy. From my place on the floor, I
didn't know if they were rummaging and stealing, or just searching. But they all spread throughout my house in an instant, as
though they each knew right where they should go. I crawled
from the front hallway, making my way to a phone in an adjoin-
ing room. I punched in 9-1-1 and when I heard the receiver lift,
I began my plea for help. But my call was intercepted by one of
the little children on another extension in another room. The
child's voice on the other end just laughed. At that moment I
knew that I was powerless, totally at the mercy of my intruders.*

Deeply troubled, I woke from my sleep. I was certain that
someone had broken into our house. I was frightened. The digi-
tal clock on the stand next to my bed read 3:07. I got out of the
bed and, in darkness, began to search the house for prowlers.

All of us house within ourselves a "sanctum sanctorum," a
place so mysterious and so holy that even we, ourselves, are usually afraid to enter it – at least while we're awake and in control.
But this is the place in which God dwells.

This second part of my story delves into my spiritual journey,
where I seem to mostly loiter around at the threshold of that sacred place within me. Whereas the tales from the food pantry of
St. Peter Claver Church reveal some of the ongoing outward
struggles of the Church's urban ministry, this tale reveals some
of the ongoing inward struggles of my search for God.

I have a lot of inward struggles. Most of my current ones
involve life and work in the inner city – the heart of Kansas City,
in the heart of America.

I decided to become a priest several times in my life. The
first time was as a child, when I decided to become many things.
The last time was earlier in the week. But I think that the most
important time occurred when I was a seminarian, contemplating whether to stay or leave the seminary.

It was then that I met Jim LaChance, "Fr. Jim" to me at the time.

Now we both live in the same house with another priest. The house is near the places where we now work.

In my seminary days, Jim was still working at Mary Immaculate Parish, a large, wealthy suburban Catholic community that has served as a training ground for many newly ordained priests.

He is one of the few people who calls me "Tom." That is because our pastor, Monsignor O'Hara did. I never corrected them. To just about everyone else on earth who knows me, I am Thomas, the name used in my home while growing up, the name used in my schools and by all my teachers, friends and acquaintances. "Thomas, be nice to your little sister!" "Thomas, how could you get an 'F' in Religion?" "Thomas, the Dean of Students wants to see you regarding allegations of hazing at the frat house!"

But at Mary Immaculate, I was a long way from sibling squabbles, elementary faith formation, and college pranks. I had arrived at the place of discovering what it means to be a man of faith.

There are two reasons why Mary Immaculate Parish was a good training ground for me, for Jim, and for many other young priests. The first reason is that the people there had experienced a healthy transition following the Second Vatican Council. In those days, many strong Catholic communities were confused and suffered through the aftermath of that cataclysmic Council, coupled with national and world events that tore their reality apart. They had to contend with the assassination of political leaders, the Vietnam War, the Watergate Scandal, rock music, a man on the moon, hippies, and the first wave of a massive drug culture. In spite of the cultural climate, Mary Immaculate Church greeted the ecclesial changes with tremendous optimism. The parish leaders focused upon making the Church relevant in the lives of their families, who so badly needed it to be relevant.

The second reason is that they had a tremendous pastor who led them through the good times and the bad.

Monsignor Matthew O'Hara had been their shepherd from the early 1960s until his death, five years ago. In the thirty years of his pastorate, he had time to know them all and love them all, time to embrace them and let them flourish beyond his embrace. He used his time well.

As I hinted to you already, I was in the seminary when I first met Monsignor O'Hara and Jim. The Bishop had asked Monsignor to take this "certain seminarian for one summer and let him see what the life of a priest might be like." He told Monsignor that "the boy seems confused, unsure that he can offer his life to God through a priestly vocation."

Bishop charged O'Hara with this task because he knew that the good Monsignor was a man who enjoyed the vocation to which he had committed his life, the same vocation that I was contemplating at the time.

"Monsignor O'Hara," he said, "I've asked you many times to take on extra duties, and you've always generously obliged me. I don't know if the boy has what it takes or not. But before he turns his back on the seminary, and before we turn our back on the investment we've made in him, I'd like you to show him how fulfilling your life has been because you chose to serve God as a priest for all these years. However it turns out for Hartigan, I won't be disappointed."

Monsignor couldn't refuse the Bishop – he simply never did. He'd say, "it's part of my job description to obey him."

Besides that, he knew that our Bishop was right. O'Hara did love the priesthood, and it was evidenced in everything that he did.

He also didn't ever pass on an opportunity to encourage a young person to discern God's calling of him or her to discover the way, the truth, and the life. O'Hara knew that all young men and women had the answers that they look for concealed inside of them, but rarely did they know how to ask the questions in ways that those answers could be revealed to them.

I had a decent summer with the old man, or in Monsignor's words to me, "Son, you did mighty fine."

Jim LaChance got transferred to a different parish in the course of that summer, while Monsignor O'Hara and I were busy tending to all of his obligations of work and pleasure. For O'Hara, it was difficult to tell which was which. He lived by the old adage that "if you find a job you enjoy doing, you'll never have to work a day in your life." Work and pleasure flowed from one another within him, as though God really did call him to this particular way of life from his mother's womb.

Monsignor helped me to discover that the reason I pursued the priesthood from the seminary till now is simply because I seek a deeper relationship with God, and I can find that relationship best by sharing it with others. In some ways I think that my relationship with God grew deeper only because my friendship with O'Hara did. We spent several hours of every day together.

What O'Hara didn't tell the Bishop, but what I am certain that the Bishop already anticipated and calculated in, was that the old man's arthritis had gotten worse. And he knew that the senior priest would benefit from having another young companion in the parish rectory to help him get around with a little more ease.

Monsignor was seventy-eight years old then. Most of his contemporaries had retired ten to twenty years before that summer. Or they had died. O'Hara wanted to work as long as he could, and the Bishop graciously honored his desire, allowing him to remain as head of the community that had become so precious to him.

Monsignor and I hit it off very well. He was like a grandfather to me. My own grandfather had died the year I entered seminary. Jim said that it was obvious how I searched for a replacement.

At that time, almost twelve years ago, I possessed a strong need to be needed. Jim told me that, like most young priests, he once had that need, too. And like most young priests, he got over it quickly. My needs have shifted, too, as each of ours does. I suppose my chief need now is to love and be loved. Jim's is probably to be competent and respected for his competency. Monsignor informed me about all these different needs during the different stages of the priesthood.

He told me about many things. From the beginning, he treated me as a worthy disciple.

When I was ordained, two years later, the Bishop approached Monsignor again. "Matt, could you accept him as an assistant and continue the good work you've already begun with him?"

O'Hara was glad to do both.

As we two priests of Mary Immaculate went just about everywhere together and talked over just about everything, I served as his crutch, physically. He was mine socially and spiritually. Monsignor was in all of his glory privileged to transform another novice into a man of God, which, in his mind, simultaneously meant a man for the people.

He fed me sustenance that he reasoned could sustain me for life. He encouraged me to constantly explore ways that would allow God to work through me. He challenged me to become a person of prayer because, as he instructed, "only if you pray will you earn the right to talk to others about God."

We became intimate, like two musicians playing a duet, or two athletes playing a team sport, anticipating each other's moves, knowing each other's style, appreciating each other's gifts. He was easy for me to love. From him, I learned that love is an action more than a thought or a feeling, that it is a verb more than a noun.

It didn't seem like much time passed before the aging pastor began to slow down noticeably, becoming more and more dependent upon me, his young protègè, to be ever at his side. Every part of the old body was reaching the end of its service to him.

Monsignor O'Hara was in his eighty-fifth year of life and sixtieth year of priesthood when he died. He spent those final weeks in his room, where his rectory bed became his deathbed. Parishioners knelt in vigil outside the door to his room, and in the Church, praying day and night during those last seven days of their shepherd's earthly life.

For the past thirty years he had been like the angel Clarence, in *It's A Wonderful Life.* He had the ability to make each person he knew think that the world would be in shambles without them around. During those long, final hours, each of them wondered what kind of a world theirs would be without him.

Most of my time during those seven days was spent at the bedside of my teacher. I didn't want to leave, and O'Hara told me that he didn't want me to go. I didn't want to lose him and feared that I wouldn't know how to function as a person of faith for others if he wasn't present to show me. The old Monsignor spoke to me with compassion and concern for my future, as though he had chosen me to carry out a mission that he, himself, had not yet fully accomplished. Over and over again, he asked me to read to him the story of Jesus' Passion, telling the events of his final days.

The week after the funeral of my pastor and friend, I was presiding at a weekday Mass in the early morning. There were only about twenty people present, scattered throughout the Church. I saw Monsignor O'Hara kneeling among them.

When I finally had the guts to share my vision with Jim, he said, "You Irish are very peculiar. You're apt to see and hear ghosts, fairies, leprechauns, and glimpses of other worlds at any unpredictable time."

We, Irish, weren't invited to touch, though.

Of course that was the problem of my scriptural namesake. He wanted to grasp it all. While every disciple lacked faith, only "doubting Thomas" earned his dubious reputation, because he was compelled to touch. He certainly wasn't very Irish, though.

All in all, I'm sure that the Irish have some good traits, too. We enjoy stories and drink and song. We relish hearty laughter and accept sentimental tears. But others, like my friend, Jim, fault us for "taking those charisms far too seriously...as well as the religious convictions of your forebears, and the holy ghosts who visit you from the dead."

But I guess that's about the way it goes with the dead. The body gets buried, back to the earth from which it was made. The soul gets taken to the kingdom beyond, to exist under God's care, a care that judges most finally...and that loves most fully. And the spirit, in some mysterious way, remains behind to guide, to inspire and to encircle those whose eyes and ears are open to receive its lingering presence.

I didn't go back to bed after the "wake up call" I received at 3:07 in the morning. Instead, I just sat in a chair downstairs waiting for the sun to rise. There I contemplated many things, including my upcoming breakfast with Mary Kate Sullivan.

She is a college senior at Georgetown, visiting for a second "spring break," which she created into her schedule so that she could spend most of a week's time with her family. She wanted to spend it with them because, after graduation (only a month away) she would be going to Israel to teach Palestinian children through a volunteer program for which she had been chosen.

She was in junior high at Mary Immaculate Grade School the year that I was ordained and assigned there. The Sullivan family, great friends of Monsignor O'Hara for several generations, invited me in to their family's inner circle. We became close. Like

99

many pastors of large parishes with schools, Monsignor gave his youngest associates the jobs of visiting the school everyday, occasionally giving the teachers a break from their classrooms, coaching a few of the athletic teams, coordinating the youth organizations, and overseeing the Confirmation programs for teenagers. Pastors assume that their priest-associates naturally possess lots of energy to keep up with the younger parishioners. And parents certainly appreciate it any time that a priest takes interest in the lives of their family members. Mary Kate has four brothers and two sisters. She is the middle child.

As an elementary school student, she was cute, clever, athletic, intelligent and unusually considerate of others. As a young woman, she is beautiful, brilliant, deeply spiritual, and still very concerned for the welfare of others. Many young men yearn to be in her company.

She also sparks a passion within me, which causes me to remember a particular romance that I had while still in college. As I sat in our living room during the wee hours of the morning, I regretted, once again, that that college relationship was too short-lived and that I didn't pursue it to deeper levels that would satisfy my longing, even sixteen years later.

When Jim came downstairs for a cup of coffee after his alarm clock woke him at the usual time of six o'clock, I wanted to talk with him about my dream, as well as some of these thoughts inspired by it.

This dream of being robbed bothered me more at six o'clock than it did at 3:07. To me it was real. It was as real as Jacob wrestling with God's angel (or was it a devil?) through that night which he spent anticipating the reunion with his twin brother. In that case, the dreamer did get to touch and, of course, Jacob was marked for life because of it. His name and his destiny were forever changed. It was as real as Abraham and Sarah receiving the mysterious visitor(s) from some other world, who would change their fate as well. It was as real as the Astrologers from the East who had a dream – all of them – instructing them to travel by another route. My dream, like their dream, was too real.

At that hour, it was a real mysterious journey that I was taking. It was like reading the beginning of Luke's Gospel; it starts with several journeys, several visions, and several mysteries. But they weren't presented to be solved by the readers. They were presented to be accepted by them.

Jim didn't see me at first, and when he looked, the still dark scene startled him. I hadn't gone back upstairs since my original descent. Instead, I just sat there in my flannel boxers and a gray Notre Dame T-shirt. I had a baseball bat propped up against my chair. Jim, still drowsy, got his coffee, and sat down on the couch to listen to me.

"LaChance, why do you think the Roman Curia thought Pius the twelfth was nuts when he let them know that he had received apparitions from Jesus and Mary?" I asked the question while staring straight ahead.

"Because those things don't happen that often, I guess." He was asking more than answering, probably more interested in why I would care about such a thing.

"I think it happens a lot more than people admit."

"Maybe," he responded.

He mentioned to me once that another priest, a friend of his, once told him that when he was young, the Mother of God appeared to him. It was nothing spectacular. She didn't do anything or say anything to him. No one else was around to see what he saw. He knew that he couldn't verify it for skeptics, so he never told anyone about it till he mentioned it to Jim and the other members of their priest's prayer group. Then the visionary priest added that, if any of the group repeated his secret, and it got back to him, he would deny that it happened.

When Jim told me that story many months ago, it was in re-action to my revealing to him how Monsignor had appeared to me in my dreams and even while I was awake. I think I scared him. That's when he told me about his friend's apparition of Mary when he was a child. Jim may have been recalling that story as we spoke early in the morning.

I continued with my questions, which must have been re-ceived more like a stream of disconnected ramblings.

"Do you remember the play that Shaw wrote about Joan of Arc? She told her spiritual director that God spoke to her. And he said, 'That's not God, that's your imagination.' What kind of a spiritual director makes those kind of judgmental statements? Do you remember how Joan gave it back to him?"

I paused, but really didn't intend for him to give an answer.

"Vaguely..." he started to respond.

I interrupted. "She said, 'Of course it's my imagination – how else do you think God talks to us?' I always liked that come-back."

"I don't think Joan became a saint because of her imagina-tion."

"It seems to me that whatever we imagine, it eventually be-comes real on one level or another."

Jim had told me one time that I have a vivid imagination. He likes to tease me that all of the ghosts scurrying around in my mind can be blamed on my heritage. In the course of our dia-logue he probably confirmed in his head what he had earlier sus-pected from his sensory data: that I had had another strange dream or another strange vision that will haunt me a little bit more. Or I will try to convince him that it will "deepen my spiritual rela-tionships."

When I first informed Jim that Monsignor O'Hara had ap-peared in my dreams, he reasoned that "that is probably not all that abnormal since the two of you had been so close." But he also commented that I have to open myself up to such appear-

102

ances for them to occur or for them to continue.

This early morning conversation between us was not so odd as it may seem. For the past couple of years in which Jim and I shared the same house, occasionally I attempted to articulate my fears, as well as my hopes and my dreams. I realized that they would lose their power over me once I talked about them. We both agreed that we should try to voice our experiences, even if we could never share them fully or accurately.

"Jim, do you ever read any stuff by Carl Jung," I asked, "or about him?"

"Not since I was in school. Not for a long time."

He said that he didn't remember too much about Jung, but recalled that he thought him smart to break away from Freud when he did because, as he intimated, Freud was headed over the edge.

"He came up with some interesting insights about spiritual relationships, didn't he?" Jim mused.

"I think he was really onto something when he unraveled some of the mysteries of the conscious and unconscious states of being human," I told him. "He used the ocean as an image for the collective unconscious, washing up against the shores of our individual islands of consciousness. There is so much to know out there in the vast ocean of what exists. We are aware of so little of it."

Jim adopted the image I was using: "I guess sometimes those waves have to pound against our shores pretty hard to infiltrate our thick skulls and our hard hearts."

He was aware of the direction I was going. In our work we both come up against our fair share of thick skulls and hard hearts. But he was directly referring to me with that comment.

"Don't you think that our dead friends, parents and grandparents have some kind of an existence out there still?" I asked. But when he didn't respond immediately, I continued. "I think they're present more than just as figments in our minds. They're really a part of us. People come in and out of our lives so quickly sometimes, but I don't think that's the way it's supposed to be.

"It's like snow that falls, looks great for a little while, causes trouble for some people, then melts away and is gone for good. Or the flowers that grow every spring – they bring a little joy and beauty to our surroundings. But I can't even remember what those flowers in our front yard look like unless they're in bloom. Sometimes I forget what Danny looked like, and it makes me mad that I can't remember."

Danny Griffin was a friend of mine from college who died suddenly after a car accident almost two years ago.

"Tom, why do you think O'Hara stays with you? What do you still need to learn from him?" What he meant was, "Why do you let him haunt you?"

"I don't know."

After a brief pause, I started up again. "I had a weird dream this morning, LaChance. In it I had to be overpowered by a messenger who wanted to deliver something to me, something that I even wanted to receive. I've been sitting here thinking about it, wrestling with it. I think he is somehow connected to my having this dream."

And then I told Jim about the encounter I had with my own mind – or my tapping into some collective mind – while sleeping.

Somewhere I had read or heard that all of the characters in our dreams are merely different aspects of us, and that houses are symbols for our souls. So I concluded that during the night I came up against my shadow side, creeping in the darkness outside of me, and then I met up with my inner child, who laughed at my predicament from deep inside. They overtook me, and I fell to their mercy.

"The thing I'm having trouble with though," I stated after telling him the dream, "is what it is that's being delivered to me by the big guy."

104

"Tom, this is typical of you. Why do you want to try to uncover something profound here, when maybe your mind is trying to tell you something as simple as 'don't forget to alarm the house before you go to bed at night'?" He didn't say that to make me angry, though he presumed it would. He said it to encourage me to lighten up. But my look threw a dagger his way.

"But what's really typical of you is your ambivalence," he continued. "You want to both receive what's getting delivered and, at the same time, you're afraid to receive it. You usually try to fight that which is going to help you, maybe even save you."

"In that case," I mumbled pensively, "I know what it is I'm being robbed of, and I know what's being offered to me. And you're right. I am afraid of it...in the same way that I'm afraid of God."

The House Mates

3

The house we live in, a single-family-dwelling that was donated to our Diocese many years ago, is located about two miles from St. Peter Claver Church and not much farther from the two parishes that Jim serves. Unfortunately for him, the two are in opposite directions. Andy Lucca is our third housemate. He has been ordained for about thirteen years, a few more than I have and a couple less than Jim.

Andy is a high school teacher during the weekdays and serves as a supply priest to parishes on weekends. He periodically alters his name from Andrew to Drew or Andy, or even Andre, depending on his fluctuating self-esteem or his mercurial mood shifts. Once he even went through a brief phase in which he would only answer to the name "De." To his students, however, he is never anyone other than Fr. Lucca, which they always call him to his face.

He is a character in a generation of priests that has few. He continually complains of being overworked, underpaid, never appreciated and always stressed out. Regardless, he claims that God is blessing him with the conditions of affliction that he feels. His typical response to the question "how are you?" is to frown and say, "I'm stressed..." and then perk up and continue, "...but I'm blessed!" He tends to be rather histrionic and sometimes he puts his arms down to his side for the initial report and then lifts them in the air, hands open and fingers apart, for the finale of his statement of personal well being.

Though students make fun of him, as they do many teachers, he doesn't care. He also doesn't know. But what fascinates me, and Jim, and other church leaders – just about everyone else who knows him, in fact – is how much his students really like him. The churchgoers at our parishes like him, too. He is approachable, fun, easy-going and non-judgmental – seemingly rare qualities in the presbyterate.

Andy suffers from manic-depressive bouts, but he even accepts that unfortunate condition with a good attitude. On some days he is "depressed, but blessed" and on others he is "happily obsessed and divinely finessed!"

He enjoys counseling those who come to him for advice, but hasn't the foggiest idea of what he is doing. Nor does he realize the seriousness with which those individuals receive his advice. He is free of cares, by choice, and rather shallow by even high school students' standards.

He usually puts little thought into what he says to councilees – sort of like with his homilies to parishioners. He labels people's problems for them, as though he is labeling new diseases. Once he arrives at a name for their problem, his clients discover that their session is suddenly over. He abruptly stands up and announces the problem and instructs his clients to "resolve to evolve." Then he dismisses the person(s) with a promise to pray for him or her or them. As they exit, he also dismisses their problem from his mind and never again thinks about praying for them.

Their spiritual or emotional condition always ends with the word "dysfunction." For example, many of his students suffer from "household dysfunctions," which are rooted in their family systems. Some of the high school girls have "internal jealousy dysfunction;" the poorer athletes suffer from "gym coordination dysfunction" and the students with low grades have "brain atrophy dysfunction." Much of the school population and many others who know him and his competency in counseling refer to his classroom and office as "Dysfunction Junction." Overused terms and phrases that most counselors despise are always welcomed and promoted there by Andy.

In spite of his quirks, he is a good housemate. We are able to balance a respect for each other's privacy with a comfort in each other's company. Because of our schedules, we rarely eat meals together, pray our daily "Office" together, or vacation together. We are not a family, nor even a religious community – just three guys who happen to be working in the same area and decided to live together to save our employers the added expense of separate housing. At each of the three former rectories, we rent out space to increase revenues for our financially deficient parish communities.

Jim is in his seventh, and last, year of serving in the inner city. Andy and I, very soon, will be assigned the additional job of pastoring one of his parishes in addition to our current tasks. The priest shortage in our Diocese is that real, and the urban ministries often seem to suffer most because of it.

Andy usually leaves the house around seven-thirty each morning. As his blessed self bounded down the stairs on that particular morning, he must have listened for a moment before entering the living room where we sat.

Jim and I were talking about the symbolism behind Jacob wrestling with God in the night in anticipation of the reunion with his twin brother. We were discussing how it related to

108

Gandhi's insight that the only devils running around are those in our own minds, where our battles need to be fought.

"Well, somebody didn't sleep well, I can tell!" he announced from the doorway.

We said our "good mornings" to him, but were careful about asking how he was or any other question to which we might regret hearing his response. So we continued our discussion until Andy interrupted again.

"Jim LaChance, stop encouraging his nocturnal r.e.m. dysfunctions. I've got plenty of sleeping pills for all of us."

And with that, he turned from the room to toast his pop-tarts, a daily enterprise every bit as serious for him as the spiritual battles of good and evil that were fighting for possession of my soul. As God and the devil wage their war in the hearts of human beings who yearn for answers from holy guides, Andy remains oblivious to the struggle.

He is probably better off.

Though Jim and I, each, had places to be that morning, he was careful not to walk away from what was obviously very important to me.

"When you hid in the dream and peeked out into the darkness, you were sort of like John of the Cross who realized that, in the darkness, he would finally discover true light?" he asked. "Maybe that's what is happening with this turmoil you're experiencing. You're trying to look outside of yourself when you should be looking inside. You even called nine-eleven when you were asleep, and now you want to talk it out with me when you're awake, when maybe you ought to follow the mystics' ways."

"Oh yeah, those guys must have had terrific lives," I remarked sarcastically. "I wouldn't want to suffer like that, LaChance."

"It seems to me like you're making yourself suffer anyway. Don't blame it on dead people, or on some kind of altered reality that seeps out of other people's psyches. Stop beating yourself up."

I didn't get upset by, or object to, his comments – which probably surprised him. "I just think I'm supposed to learn something from this," I responded calmly. "When human and divine come together it is greater than ourselves, and I want to unravel it. Thanks for helping." I was truly grateful for his generous ear. Then I added, "but I'm not done with it yet."

Jim knew me well enough to agree that I wasn't.

My impulse is to fear something (or Someone) because of the mysterious, pervasive, presence of God. It is as if "Judgment Day" isn't going to be one day in the future, as much as it is going to be each day (and night) in brief segments, like the segment of judgment that had been handed down through my most recent state of sleep.

It's as if the decision-maker is not only God, the Judge, but also me, the defendant. I don't think that I am meant to remain passive in this judgment. But what is it that I am supposed to be deciding?

"Tom, do you remember that line from the Hebrew scriptures: 'Fear of the Lord is the first stage of wisdom?'"

I nodded.

"I remember one of my professors in seminary telling our class that we ended up with a rather poor translation of its meaning," he continued. "He said 'fear of the Lord' could be better understood as 'faith in God' or 'standing in awe.' And 'wisdom' would be better translated into our English as 'fulfillment.' Whatever fear, or awe, you currently feel is probably really mystical faith, and it will probably lead to fulfillment if you're patient with it."

I was intrigued by his insight. For early in the morning, LaChance was making sense. And, I decided he really does believe what he told me. We can't get around our issues, as so many of us try. We've got to trudge right through them instead.

"If the doors of perception were cleansed..." I pensively began these often-quoted words of William Blake, even though I usually credit them to Jim Morrison.

"...We would see reality as it truly is: infinitc," Jim completed the sentence.

I, like Morrison and Blake and so many other sojourners before us, approach the doors hoping to view some of the mysteries of the universe and beyond – some of the majesty of the individual conscious and the collective unconscious. I would pursue onward with great respect for the mystery of it all.

Our buddy, Andy, must have been listening from his breakfast table in the kitchen, both to our words and to my thoughts. He stopped at the doorway leading outside and, in a mocking voice of the "Toy Story" astronaut, shouted out: "To infinity... and beyond!"

With that, we heard the door slam and determined that it was a good time to squelch this dialogue and face the day ahead.

When Andy dashed out the door, his shoe nearly came down over the top of a caterpillar that was crawling across the sidewalk. He caught himself just before squishing the insect in certain, sudden death. Adjusting his step, he managed to hop over it. As he slid into his little cherry-red Plymouth Sundance to drive away, the unknowing, furry creature crawled along from the sidewalk to the grassy lawn. The sticker on Andy's back bumper could only be read at a very close distance: "In a world of minor lunacy the actions of both the wholly sane and the totally deranged appear equally odd."

Mary Kate's Journey

4

While I consumed a full breakfast of bacon, eggs, hash browns, toast and coffee, Mary Kate ordered a bagel, of which she ate less than half. We remained at the restaurant for nearly two hours. Typical of our conversations, this one was not dull. We didn't experience those uncomfortable silent moments that sometimes occur in human interaction, nor do either of us have a need to prepare back-up dialogue in our minds, just in case the audible one isn't going anywhere.

Even though we are fifteen or sixteen years apart in age, we are good friends. Mary Kate is incredibly mature, knowledgeable about civic issues and international concerns, and deeply thoughtful about her opinions, which are always well informed and springing from a spiritually based value system that her family teaches and lives. I hold her in high admiration.

She is one of the few people from the suburban parishes who knows me and also understands that my getting assigned to the inner city was not a demotion, nor a punishment. So many of them think that I must have done something that the Bishop didn't like. They feel sorry for me during my "exile."

Rarely do I return to the social circles of Mary Immaculate Parish.

The last time I had seen Mary Kate was when her family invited me to join them for dinner during the Christmas Season. Her current boyfriend, also a Georgetown senior but from the New England area, was present on that winter evening. Nick is his name and, as you might expect, he is handsome, tall, athletic, witty, very bright, and able to charm the entire Sullivan family.

Mary Kate looked so beautiful against the holiday background. Her long brown hair with the red tint framed her perfect face. Her smile glowed, accentuating her loveliness. I was envious of Nick and the ways in which they touched and interacted. Though I probably could have gotten away with making a joke about my jealousy, I dared not. It is not so much that I need to hide my feelings from Mary Kate or from the Sullivans as much as it is that I need to hide them from myself. So many people prefer that good, holy priests not have such feelings. Sometimes I wanted to elevate myself to their preference.

There is a big difference between admiring, even loving, another and reacting to impulses and urges. Many people I know, priests included, rather than deal with their feelings, choose to ignore every person they encounter out of fear for what love can be.

As alluring as Mary Kate had looked that night four months earlier, she was even more stunning at our morning rendezvous. Hers is a natural beauty that is brought to life by her mannerism and emphasized by her humility. In a way, I'm sure that I had no business spending time with her that morning, even though it had been her request that we meet.

She wanted to talk about her year ahead, about the Holy Land, about the richness of the religions that were born there, about the Jewish lobby in Washington, DC, about the Palestinians who suffer, about the children she would be teaching. She wanted to discuss her vocation and how she is searching to make her life meaningful to others. And to herself. And to her God.

"Father Thomas, I'm anxious about the year ahead and the choices I'm facing. I know it was smart to turn down the offers from those companies, at least for now. I know that I want to take a break from school, too, though I wouldn't mind returning for advanced studies a year or two down the road. Nick and I really care for each other. He's so unique, so different from any guy I've dated before. It will be very difficult for us to be apart next year. And, believe it or not, I still want to offer my life to God and serve others, maybe even become a nun."

This was not the first time that I heard her say the part about being a nun, and I was surprised every time. This was no exception. And I was more surprised still because, as she talked about it, I realized that she was serious.

For her sake, I wish that greater options existed in the Church's institutional structure for young, bright, gifted, deeply spiritual women, who are natural leaders. Though many religious women have many of these attributes, the greater option, as most of us Catholics have been taught since our first catechism class, is ordination to the priesthood. Not to take anything away from the burdens of our office, it also presents a priviledge that is not offered to non-ordained females.

As she spoke about her senior year in college, I recalled my own. All of my friends seemed to know exactly what they wanted then. It was the dawn of the eighties. They all wanted money. They all wanted power. Though I was confused about what I wanted as my graduation approached, I was not confused about what I didn't want. I didn't want what they were after. I didn't want to get lost in the corporate world. I didn't want to continue the dating games. I was tired of the fraternity parties, the bars, and the meaningless relationships with the girls with whom I went out, relationships that never lasted very long. I had fun during those years and was glad about it, for that had been my primary objective as a college student. But in my final semester, I became so angry with myself because I, among all of my classmates, had lost my sense of direction. Or did I ever even have one?

After graduating, I accepted a job at my new alma mater, still seemingly unable to find my way. I was living in the same area close to the campus, frequenting the same bars, hanging with the same students and former students, some graduates and some drop-outs.

But after a year of that mundane cycle, I found myself in the seminary for the simple reason that I wanted to "get it out of my system." I wanted to be able to say to someone (or Someone) later that I had seriously considered the priesthood at one time in my life. Probably I remained in the seminary for too long. But I didn't leave because I determined that I had finally found something meaningful – intrinsically meaningful to me and potentially meaningful to others.

"Is that where Mary Kate is now?" I wondered.

No. It can't be. There are so many differences between me and her, so many differences between then and now. So much seems to have changed in the decade and a half between our final years of college.

For starters, Mary Kate and her friends are so much more healthy and focused. They don't drink alcohol, or not much. They don't "experiment" with drugs. They don't desire unnecessary material things. They crave simplicity and what is natural. They want to reach out to others. They pursue meaningful relationships. And they seek to understand their purpose within the universe. It seems much more profound than what MTV might have us believe.

During my college days, I read Ayn Rand and thought that I understood her philosophy, even thought that I wanted to buy into it. Mary Kate, on the other hand, was reading Fydor Dostoevsky and discerning how she could help bring about the redemption for which his words longed. The difference put simply is that my friends, with whom I surrounded myself, were iconoclasts and hers are humanitarians.

I listened to her speak about her vocational opportunities and I shared some of my own experiences in making choices. She came to me as a priest and as a friend. My intent was to be both. To my own satisfaction, I succeeded.

"It doesn't matter which lifestyle you end up choosing Mary Kate. The only thing that matters is the attitude in which you live it out. Married, single, or religious, you can be great in whichever vocation you choose. And whatever you end up doing for a career, I know you'll use your talents to benefit others and you'll create a better world for those you're going to meet and influence."

She gets easily embarrassed. And my compliment embarrassed her. She smiled and lifted a hand toward her forehead to smooth her hair, brushing the strands which had fallen around her face to the back of her head.

"I guess," she started, "I'd just like God to be a little more clear with me."

She, too, is in search of a dream. She can become whatever and whoever she wants. Through whatever she chooses, Mary Kate Sullivan will give glory to God and dignity to those she encounters.

"You're standing at the intersection of so many crossroads. I think you have a very clear sense of the way that will lead to your destination. Israel will help you get there. So will your interaction with the Palestinian children and their families.

"Being separated from everyone and everything you know for a year might even help. So might your relationship with Nick. You know where you're headed, Mary Kate. But what's even

116

more important than your destination is that you enjoy these experiences that take you there. I hope you can truly recognize and appreciate the opportunities available to you."

"Like everybody else in life, I just want to be happy," she responded. "But I know that where I'm searching for happiness is probably not where most other people will search for it, or find it."

Though she had hardly eaten, I noticed that our waitress kept filling up her water glass. As she sipped, I recalled a conversation that Sister Mary Ellen and I had facilitated with the Confirmation students of our inner city youth group. When we asked them who were their heroes, most of the young people listed stars from the NBA or NFL, beautiful movie stars and models, people whose common achievement was to attain wealth and leave their past behind them.

One high school student named Vincent, however, had a different response. He told us and his peers about his dad, about how dedicated his father is to his work on the railroads, how his dad sometimes holds down a second job as a carpenter, how he tries to be present for his children, how he volunteers what little free time he has to take poorer children fishing, or show them how to make simple objects out of wood.

Sister praised Vincent's choice and then told the whole group that they shouldn't put too much stock in the big names who too often turn their backs on their past. She said that eventually each of the youth would have to look inside of themselves and become their own heroes, and discover that there is so much good that they can offer to make life better for others.

Mary Kate will become a hero for somebody, much like Vincent's father is for him. As she begins that trek, I wanted to give her some sound advice that she can take along on her journey, take along in search of her dreams. But I am on a similar search myself. And I don't know if I would take my own advice in facing the choices I might have to make. I am sometimes bored with the priesthood. I am frustrated by what seems to be hopeless situations that face the inner city poor. Amongst my boredom and frustration, I entertain choices that may be difficult for me to make.

Andy had told me, "Listen, I know the signs of depression and you're depressed."

Though I appreciate his concern, I am certain that I don't suffer from clinical depression; I simply feel sorry for myself. That's all. I don't like it, and I will snap out of it. I'm just not sure how or when. The lyrics from one of Paul Simon's songs paraded through my brain: *"Breakdowns come and breakdowns go...but what are ya gonna do about it? That's what I wanna know."*

I want to do something about it.

My thoughts and feelings seem so distorted and disjointed of late. I want guidance, and I miss the constant presence of Monsignor O'Hara, who always seemed to have good answers for me. It helps to be around others, like the Sullivans, who miss him, too.

As I contemplated Mary Kate's future, so did I contemplate my own. It felt as if I was back for my final semester of college with her, and feeling the pressures of graduation's deadline all over again. I didn't usually handle deadlines very well.

Am I back in college hanging on the fence of my future, or am I hanging on the cross? The choice that faced the two thieves who hung on either side of Jesus was sublime. One chose life while the other chose death. One sought redemption while the other didn't. One went out in faith while the other still held doubts. The challenge of true discipleship is to keep choosing life, especially at our hours of death.

For sure, the one life-giving choice that I made was my choice to become a priest. But is it still giving life to me, or just sucking it away? And what is it giving to all those who I am supposed to be serving?

Perhaps the greatest of all sins is the sin of being discouraged by one's own faults and weaknesses, because that can lead to despair. In spite of myself, my work as a priest is good work. But is it good enough? Am I just a *"worthless servant"* doing *"no more than is my duty"?*

I understood that what Mary Kate meant by happiness isn't caused by things people seek – things like wealth, health, friendship and knowledge – things important in our world. The happiness she sought could not be acquired with, nor taken away by, this world's offerings.

Mary Kate, not much more than a teenager, realized what I'm only beginning to realize. She comprehends that true happiness is within us and eager to manifest itself through priceless human interaction.

At the end of our breakfast, I simply reminded Mary Kate that "travel is symbolic of search. It will be good for you to travel, see different cultures, and reverence different ways of life and different ways of relating to God. But when you have done that," I instructed her, "return home and discover that what you were searching for was with you from the very beginning. What you thirst for is the wellspring of holiness that Jesus offers internally. 'Holy Land' is a relative term. The place where you eventually settle and live will undoubtedly be holy."

My words sounded more like those of Monsignor O'Hara than my own. But I was actually thinking about the inner city, and how so many people who choose to worship in the inner cities of America do so because they believe that that is where God dwells. I, too, think that they must be some of the holiest places on earth – the places where I live among the poor, the lowly, the desolate.

When we departed from the restaurant, Mary Kate thanked me for taking the time to see her and confer some priestly advice upon her. I told her that it was my pleasure. And it was. I understood that Mary Kate trusted me for guidance, and I would not betray her trust. I lovingly supported her. I suppose that I should be embarrassed or feel guilty or confess disloyalty to my vocation for how excited and energized I am in her presence, so happy to be alive. Maybe my priest brethren would. But why? I am energized because she is at a stage in her life where I once was, but in a place beyond my old dwelling. I am excited because of her upcoming adventures and immanent offering of internal joy to those she encounters. I am attracted to her youthful beauty. And appreciation of youthful beauty cannot be wrong.

It is true that I have no control over the thoughts that enter into my mind and the feelings that enter into my heart. But I can control how I handle those thoughts and feelings. And I know it becomes wrong when the appreciation turns to desire.

Thoughts of good and evil do combat in my own mind, though. It is as if there are twins existing inside of me, two different disciplines urging two different responses. I realize that if I want to succeed in my vocation though, I will have to turn them into disciples of the truth. For I recognize that disciples who feel the forces of good and evil battling within must be self-disciplined in spiritual matters.

My relationship with Mary Kate will always remain platonic, though it cannot be captured as simply "fatherly," or summarized as purely "innocent." But I truly love her as a friend, confidante and even spiritual guide. And I wish for her happiness, her success and her faithfulness to the pursuit of her dreams.

When we pulled out of the parking lot, Mary Kate went west and I went east, back in the directions of the worlds that we had left earlier in the morning. A few blocks away, I looked out through the window on my passenger side and saw Monsignor O'Hara standing at a bus stop. He was dressed in his black "clerics," which he always wore in public. He was talking and laughing and several people were gathered around him. They looked like street people, bums, old drunks, young prostitutes. They were listening to him; they were responding, smiling and enjoying his company.

I heard a voice say to me: "Go deeper into this moment of your longing. Pray into the desire of your heart. Love will propel you to be generous to others."

The Sacraments of Vocation

5

A man and woman sat in "the office of the pastor," located in our parish's rectory. The man looked youthful as he held their child in his arms. The little girl, though she could walk, sat calmly in his embrace and watched me – the pastor – as I directed the conversation of her parents. I knew the woman quite well: Johnette Sawyer is an active member of St. Peter Claver. She was here with her boyfriend, Aarion, to talk with me about getting married at the church – her church. Neither of them appeared to be nervous.

I, on the contrary, always dread these conversations. The Catholic Church has prohibitive rules about marriage that should discourage most inquirers from ever contemplating a religious ceremony. But it rarely works. The Church is crazy to be in the wedding business at all, I think, not to mention the annulment business.

It causes so much confusion for both Catholics and non-Catholics. I try to explain to couples who discuss the subject with me, that the Church is not really interested in weddings, only in sacramental marriages. Their responses usually indicate that they don't think there is a difference. It is understandable, however, why such couples aren't interested in broadening their focus beyond the wedding ritual. In their minds, that is why they are supposed to come and see a priest.

Couples typically contact churches with a previously determined wedding date clearly etched in their minds, and they inquire as to what hoops they would have to jump in order to have a church ceremony that can precede their reception – already booked at a particular club or hall. They always jump through whatever hoops we give them. I've come to think that a marriage should not be referred to as a Sacrament at the time of the wedding. For several reasons, I hold this conviction.

Foremost is that the majority of engaged couples are ill prepared. I attended six years of preparation in two seminaries in order to become a priest. There is no claim from the Church that my Sacrament of Ordination is, in any way, more sacred than their Sacrament of Matrimony. Yet their four-month notice is certainly not equal to my six-year formation program. It isn't that I think that the demands of the seminary system are too much to require either.

Quite the contrary, I suspect that even more preparation would have been good for me, as it would for other priests I know. Rather, it seems to me that the Church offers a tremendous disservice to couples seeking sacramental marriages by asking them to jump through those few hoops against the deadline of their wedding day. If it were up to me, sacramental preparation for marriage would begin sometime in high school when the search for a life-long partner begins for some.

What I really think is unfair, though, is that only these two vocational lifestyles are even sacramentalized by the Church while two others – the avowed life of religious women and men and the single life – are more or less ignored.

Johnette is the type of person who I didn't want to discourage. She is thirty-eight years old, a faithful member of our church community, and a strong example in so many ways. But her situation, though seemingly typical within the African-American community, is full of problems for the Roman rules-makers and the rules-enforcers.

That's probably why so many African-American Catholics relate to the Church in the same way that they relate to American society. There is a sense that civic and religious leaders keep telling them that they belong to the mainstream, but also keep acting like they don't. The obvious result is that blacks receive mixed messages from the words and deeds of white leaders.

Johnette is viewed by other Catholics at St. Peter Claver as a leader within our community. Her children – she has four more than the toddler, plus one grandchild – are well known, well behaved, and well respected by others. Johnette makes sure that they are in church every Sunday. They consistently participate in service work like neighborhood clean-ups, social events like receptions after Masses, and educational programs like Sunday school. They are talented and they use their talents to benefit others. She is one of the leaders who I attempt to elevate as an example for our community, but my doing so appears to ignore the mores of our religion.

Johnette had never married simply because she had never loved any of the men she dated prior to Aarion – not even the fathers of her other children. Her oldest daughter, Teresita, is twenty, and has a child of her own. Teresita's father, a child himself when she was born, has never been a part of her life. The father of Johnette's twelve-year-old son and the twin boys – now ten – is in their lives though. And their mother is glad. He sends money, goes to their ball games and spends time with them periodically. At no time did he or she want to marry the other. But Johnette did want to be a mother. And she proves to be a good one, a very good one. He didn't mind making babies with her even though he remains on the periphery of their lives. Many white people seem to look down on arrangements such as these, but the two of them are fine with it. It doesn't matter to them like it does to me – probably another righteous ideal of which I need to let go.

Aarion and Johnette have dated one another during the previous five years. He has lived with her and her children for the past two, moving in soon after their daughter was born. Aarion is seven years younger than Johnette. He has two daughters of his own by two different women. His older child was born when he and the girl were sixteen – sophomores in high school. They never considered marriage as an option. He did, however, consider marrying his younger child's mother. But that thought faded when she married another man without warning Aarion.

In both cases, though, he dutifully accepted his paternal responsibilities. As much as he is permitted, he remains in the lives of his children with whom he spends most of his free time. His two girls like the Sawyer family and want to be with them whenever they can. That makes their dad very happy.

The man and woman want to get married at this point in their lives because they think it is important to ritualize their commitment to one another in front of their families and friends, and they want to live the rest of their lives as husband and wife. They are joyful people who approach life with enthusiasm. They each possess a good sense of humor and a good work ethic. They have problems, mostly financial, but they make necessary sacrifices to survive their problems. Children are not a problem. Her children respect him and are enriched by his fatherly presence, though it is clear that she calls the shots when it comes to the children. She is better at it.

I adjusted my presentation on marriage to better fit the situation at hand. I skipped over my routine on the evils of premarital sex, but still informed them of how the Church upholds the sacredness of human sexuality and sexual acts that are to be reserved to the marital union.

After gaining the pertinent information from them, I referred to the four aspects of Christian marriages, and asked that their marriage also be unitive, procreative, exclusive and permanent in accord with the Church.

"The unitive aspect of marriage ties your love for one another with God's love for you and for each of us. In the Hebrew scriptures, God entered into a covenant relationship with his chosen people. Not a contract, but a covenant. We believe that Christ did the same with his bride, the Church, which he established in the Christian scriptures. If you marry at Peter Claver, you're essentially stating that you'll do what they did: give up your own self for the sake of the other, so that, as the Bible states, 'the two are no longer two, but one'."

My mouth was very dry, as were my words.

I didn't even believe myself when I spoke like that. I'm not sure that Jesus even intended to establish a church. Oh sure, he said, "...upon this rock I will build my church..." but did he actually intend another institution? Wasn't he referring to a way of life? Yet somehow, somewhere in history, the institutional Church – claiming to be the bride of Christ – institutionalized itself and then institutionalized marriage as well.

At this point in my spiel some couples typically interrupt to ask about lighting a unity candle. To me, the unity candle – a symbol of oneness to them – is a symbol of easy love, immature love, romantic love – another decoration to go with their banners, balloons and bountiful bridal party. But because I get frustrated by couples' focusing upon their wedding day ceremonies rather than upon their lifetime marriage commitment, I am in the habit of moving along with my presentation without pausing to give them a chance. This time was no exception.

"The procreative aspect intends that your love for one another be realized in the embodiment of your own flesh and blood – your children. Though your children may be the center of your

126

lives, they should never be the center of your marriage. As you are willing to pass along life," I nodded toward their baby, "so must you also be willing to pass along faith."

The little child still had her eyes on me, watching me. She leaned back against her daddy's chest, trusting in the security of his embrace. The child had made little noise and had done minimal tossing during the fifteen minutes in which we had been sitting. But she was very alert and tuned in to her environment.

"Father, the older I get the more important faith becomes for me," Johnette leaned forward as she spoke. She smiled as she continued, "Now I understand better why my parents forced us, beggin' and screamin' against them every Sunday, to go to church with them."

"And that's why, when we baptize a baby – as we did your Shante last year – we don't baptize the baby, foremost, into the institutionalized church. We baptize that baby, first, into the faith that you, as parents, choose to pass along to her by the home you provide and the example you give. The Church can only support the primary formation that you offer her." Then I added half jokingly, "and we're always here when parents find it necessary to force their children to more religious exposure."

"Ya know, Father, as parents we don't want you to think we got the steps of marriage put in the wrong order," Aarion wanted to be clear. "But we think we're doin' the right thing here, and we want to do it right as an example for all our children, too."

"I admire that," I cut in. "There are probably lots of stages to marriage that ought to be put in some sort of a logical order: friendship, infatuation, romance, parenting, growing up together, growing old together, companionship, falling deeper into the heart of the other and deeper into the heart of God. There are probably similar stages for the priesthood. I know they don't always happen in the right order, or at the right time. I was made a pastor after only one assignment...too soon for me. People want me to give them wisdom on topics that I haven't had the years to become wise about. I know that things don't always fall in the right order."

"Not bein' Catholic, myself, I don't know too much about your church, but I think we're gonna do the best we can," Aarion said.

He freed one of his hands from around his daughter and reached over to take Johnette's hand, which was resting on the arm of the chair next to the one in which he sat.

I decided not to go on, as I usually did, about why the Church takes a clear stand against premarital sex, extramarital sex, homosexual acts, and other forms of sex which diminish the dignity of the conjugal act of marriage. I decided not to go on, as I usually did, about common impediments to marriage like addictions to drugs and alcohol, patterns of physical and emotional abuse, and other forms of unfaithfulness between one partner and the other. I decided not to go on, as I usually did, about the many reasons that so many divorces happen in modern American society. And I decided not to offer my usual warning about how the two of them are going to change – sometimes together and sometimes apart, how they must change, how the years will change them, and how the years will change the very definition of marriage. I wanted to tell them that what is motivating them now is not what will be sustaining them later, if their marriage is to last. But I decided not to.

Instead, I got up to get a glass of water to quench my thirst.

When couples come to see me announcing their intention and engagement, I often ask them why they want to get married. One or the other usually responds that it is because they are in love. I think that love is a good thing to be in. But I sometimes wonder how long they can be in it. As I look at them I wonder if they can be in it very long if one partner makes a bad choice that breaks their marriage vow. I wonder if they can be in it long if something or someone they always counted on is suddenly gone from their lives. I wonder if they can be in it long if their offspring's defects or disappointments force them to refocus their existence.

How long, I wonder. Like many priests, I don't think that love is a good enough reason to want to get married. The desire to make a life-long commitment to another, and to children born of the union, is a better reason.

I wonder sometimes about my own promises and vows. My commitment is also to Another. I know that my commitment has changed. The priesthood to which I was ordained is not the same priesthood, which I serve. It has changed; I have changed. As I keep telling parishioners, "change is inevitable, but growth is optional."

Am I growing with the changes?

There is always joy in a union such as marriage or the avowed life, at least for a while. Especially when it's easy. But can easy, immature, romantic love grow into difficult, mature, real love in a couple's union with each other? In my union with the Church? Will my commitment survive harsh, dreadful times?

Refocusing my mind on the couple before me, I did decide to assess their abilities to communicate with one another, using a little form that a counselor-friend gave to me. The counselor told me that he could discover nearly everything he needs to know about the future of a couple by asking the right questions about their pasts. In doing so, he predicts their liabilities and problems, as well as their strengths and successes. I suppose that families-of-origin do provide a blue print for the next generation of families. So it all seems relatively logical.

As I returned with my water I decided that Aarion and Johnette would be fine – as though that is even mine to decide. I certainly didn't want to impede their union. Though I also know that with them, as with Mary Kate, as with myself, the future is up for grabs. The future, by its very definition, remains ambiguous. We can never commit ourselves to a future of ambiguity. People are better off if they simply exist in the mystery and become comfortable with the ambiguity.

My image of the little girl in the presence of her parents – the presence of comfort – listening to the strange priest, to the mysterious language about the ambiguous times ahead, is for me a rather good image for how I, and we, should address the future. Our destiny will be realized by the attitudes that we develop. If we trace these attitudes back through our habits, our actions, and our beliefs, we will probably discover that it is our value system that shapes our destiny.

I admire Johnette and Aarion. Admittedly, their standards of behavior are different from mine, as are their life experiences. But so what? They are going to do the best that they can.

Dreams Revisited

6

Several weeks later, after a long day of meetings, Jim returned home late one night. His last meeting turned out to be the longest. His appointments that day took him back and forth, to and from both of his parishes, passing a couple of blocks from our house each time he got in his car to head to his next destination. When he finally did arrive home, I was asleep on the living room sofa; I had dozed off while reading.

He didn't understand how I could sleep. A window behind the sofa was open and the typical loud street noises (sirens, revved-up engines, helicopters, car stereos, people shouting at each other – threatening and cussing...there was always plenty of threatening and cussing) blared out and entered into our living room. Van Morrison was strumming up to sing "Into the Mystic."

"We were born before the wind, also younger than the sun... let your soul and spirit fly into the mystic."

Jim was hesitant to wake me.

He figured that since much of the world is shouting "show

131

me the money" as though it is the key to happiness, and I am whispering "trust the dream" as though it is the key to eternity, I shouldn't be awakened, for I pursued the more important commodity. Jim crossed in front of me in the direction of the music on the c.d. player.

"...And when that fog horn whistle blows, I got to hear it. I don't want to fear it...then magnificently we will float into the mystic."

When he hit the "stop" button, I turned over.

"What's going on?" I asked as I sat up groggily. My legs were still stretched out across the sofa.

"A late Parish Council meeting at St. Joseph. I thought it would never end. But it's my last one, so that made it a little easier to sit through."

One of the frustrations of the priesthood for Jim and for me is that our time is not our own. Early in the morning, late into the evening, in the middle of the night sometimes, it often belongs to someone else. But I guess we realized that coming into the deal we made.

"What are you dreaming about tonight? And why aren't your dreams more like mine where you just desire to be desired by those you desire?" Jim added while walking over toward the outside noises. As he closed the window, he commented on seeing a cocoon lodged on the outside of the screen. It was covered in a silky cobweb, providing a tomb of peaceful rest for the evolving life that slept inside.

He went to the kitchen and the liquor cabinet to make a Johnny Walker on the rocks. He often enjoyed winding down with a drink and conversation.

"I wasn't dreaming, LaChance," I mumbled back and then quietly added, "or I don't remember if I was."

I was lying though, on both counts.

Before I snapped out of my sleep, the late Archbishop of Chicago had visited me in this same living room.

132

Joseph Cardinal Bernadine sat down beside me and spoke to me very personally, even lovingly. I had never met the man in my life, but I respected him from afar and admired the daring, pastoral leadership with which he gifted the Church in the United States. The late prelate said that he wanted to pass along to me three bits of advice, and hoped that I could receive them. I made a point of trying hard to remember each of them.

But when I woke up – Jim's fault – I forgot the first two. I recalled the third piece of advice, though; at least in essence I recalled it.

I remembered it because Bernardine told me that it was the most important of the three. It had to do with people – how to handle them when they disappoint us and how to love them when they frustrate us. The Cardinal made a reference to Jesus' Sermon on the Mount. He explained to me how the throngs of people in that place and time wanted so badly to make Jesus' message become a reality in their lives. But they couldn't or wouldn't, or just didn't. Many of them began with good intentions, but their motivation could not sustain them for very long.

He also told me that many people who mourn the loss of one who loved them, one who changed their lives for the good, will be inspired by the emotion of their loved one's passing, and pledge to live a different way of life filled with loving service. They will pledge to put on the attitude of Jesus. But it doesn't last with those people either. They mean well, but they are weak.

The Cardinal spoke to me with a gentle voice. I sensed his loving kindness and felt so good and honored to be in his presence. And I admired Bernardine's humility. He was an extraordinary and courageous leader in a nation and a church that doesn't seem to me to have many from that mold. He was a seeker of truth. Like Dr. Martin Luther King, Jr. before him, he wasn't afraid to dream of a better world and work toward making the dream a reality.

When I awoke and saw Jim, I imagined that he had told me we should be good to people even if they aren't good to us, even if they make us give up our evenings to stay out late attending silly meetings that usually get us absolutely nowhere.

My groggy mind drifted: ...we should be good to them...even if they make up things about us that can badly damage us...even if they plague us like a cancer, coming at us from every direction, wanting food, wanting assistance, wanting relief, wanting guidance, wanting salvation, wanting retribution for the ways in which churches and church leaders had oppressed their entire race in days gone by, wanting the things of which we cannot give anymore than we are giving.

As my friend settled down with his drink and poured a Jameson for me, he asked me the question, "What are you thinking about?"

"I was thinking: 'why is it that when I finally fall asleep, it doesn't last?'" Alert now, I asked, "Hey, Jim, do you remember when I told you that I was being assigned to Peter Claver?"

He nodded.

"Do you remember what you said?"

"Yeah. First I told you that your auto insurance would triple. Then I told you how humiliating it is for priests in the inner city to have to beg from priests in the wealthy parishes."

"Uh huh. You even quoted Simone Weil and told me how the begging exchange, no matter how hard we try to change it, always only reinforces the two roles we play: the humiliator and the humiliated." I shifted my body so that I was facing him more directly. "But that's not the part I was thinking about. You also told me that after one year here, I'd conclude that Mary Immaculate was a cold parish compared with all the warmth I would receive in the urban core. You told me that God was really present among these people."

"I'm glad you remember me telling you that," he spoke humbly. "I forgot I said it, though," he added apologetically. After a brief pause, he continued. "I kind of wish that someone from the suburbs would tell me how terrific the people there are, because I've forgotten. It would be a good thing to hear it now that I'm heading their way."

We talked for a few minutes about the many ways we have changed in recent years. We changed because we have been given the privilege to live among the less fortunate, those whom Jesus called the "anawim" (the little ones, the faithful ones). And we talked about how our sense of the priesthood has changed, too. Though Jim is ready to be reassigned, I know that he will miss the urban ministries, and even miss living here with Andy and me.

My friend LaChance was talkative, telling me how he no longer thinks of us as beggars but as proclaimers of Christ's care for the lowly. It was he who shifted the topic of our late night conversation.

"Tom, I've thought about our conversation here the other morning."

I guess it seemed to both of us like just the other morning, even though a month had passed.

"I want you to know that I agree with you that our lifestyle and vocation really depends on our having a strong relationship with God, anyway that that happens. And I concede that it can happen in many diverse ways. It can happen even if our imaginations offer us a deeper self-awareness, or reveal God's presence to us, unveiling some better understanding of our connectedness to him. That, in turn, may lead to our own self-respect and worth as ministers so that we can encourage others to do the same – that is, strengthen their relationship with God."

"Yeah, don't knock the imagination, LaChance...or the dreamer." I didn't comprehend most of what he said, but was ready to shift from light-headed words to more serious talk. "It's all over the Bible, from beginning to end. Joseph in the Old Testament...and it's Joseph again in the New. Joseph – now there was a dreamer."

I'm sure that Joseph, the husband of Mary, had nothing more reliable to count on than his dreams. Think about it. His fiancee was pregnant. The only thing that he knew, for sure, was that he wasn't the father. A couple of years later, that crazy monarch Herod started slaughtering baby boys the same age as his stepson. Both times, Joseph trusted in the dream. He had no fear about taking Mary as his wife. He quickly got his family the hell out of the holy land, too, when so instructed through his sleep.

And his troubles weren't over yet. A decade later, the child ran away from home. For three days, neither he, nor the boy's mother, knew where their son had gone.

I take advantage of opportunities to retell those stories to my parishioners, as on the Feast of the Holy Family or any other feast day in which Mary and Joseph are held up as the ideal example for modern families to follow.

Somewhere in our American history, the moral majority decided that the nuclear family is the only way to go to be politically correct and religiously right. Teenage homelessness, runaway kids, pregnancies out of wedlock, babies having babies, step-parents rearing children, other children senselessly murdered – these are all important issues among the dwellers of our inner cities. Suburbia and exurbia, too – we just don't talk about them as much out there.

I think Andy is not totally off target when he traces his client and student problems back to their family's dysfunctions. Of course, families have always been dysfunctional: remember Adam and Eve? Cain and Abel?

And what about those twelve sons of Jacob? Most of them were envious of their brother Joseph because their dad played favorites...and Joseph was "it" most of the time. They were willing to sell him into slavery. Some were even willing to leave him for dead.

Envy, malice, and other such sinful attitudes must be in our

Judeo-Christian gene pool somewhere. I guess we should work
and pray that the dominant "function" will overpower the reces-
sive "dysfunction."

I envision a parallel story with the East Coast's "College of
Cardinals," though it seems that they sometimes behave more
like a community college, or junior college – more like a fraternity of predictable members who keep replacing themselves with
more of themselves. Could they sell out their own brother? I
wondered if it ever felt that way to Bernardine who disappeared
from my dream when Jim, in the flesh, replaced him in our living
room.

I diffused my thoughts and listened to my friend. "I'll grant
you that it's throughout scripture, but I don't know about 'from
beginning to end,' Tom. The myth of the creation of Eden and
those guys in *Revelation* probably were more like your Jim
Morrison, with his kind of imagination...or his kind of drugs."
He paused for a moment and then asked the question I wanted
him to ask.

"Did you ever figure out what the big guy was wanting to
deliver to you?"

"Love." I didn't hesitate. "I knew it the morning we talked
but I was unwilling to say it then. It sort of bothered me."

"What do you mean?"

"Well that was the morning I was going to meet Mary Kate
Sullivan for breakfast," I started.

Jim knew the Sullivans from his own days at Mary Immaculate. He had listened to me speak about her on a few occasions
before this one, as we periodically discussed those whom we knew
from our novice days there. Each time we did, it became evident
to both of us that we had different memories and different per-
spectives of the same place and the same people.

Though he knew her older brothers better than he knew Mary
Kate, he recollected her as a scrawny third grader with freckles.
So I am glad that he didn't say what he was thinking. He had to

fight back laughter when I told him about our special friendship. It was more difficult for him now that I, with tremendous vulnerability, mentioned "love." I'm sure that the late hour, following lengthy meetings, didn't help the matter for him either. I chose not to look in his direction while I spoke, because I knew that he was trying to wipe the smile from his face.

I, for my part, continued with my very serious confession. "In the dream I was getting robbed of romantic love and intimacy with my beautiful partner who I will never have.

"In college I fell in love only once. I was a senior. Her name was Libby and I hardly knew her. We had gone out only two, maybe three, times. Though she didn't seem like anything special at the time, later I recognized how incredible she was: attractive, savvy, mature, bright, kind to everyone, and so self-confident – all those things I was not. I didn't realize my feelings for her until a month or two after the last time we went out together."

"What happened when you did?" Jim interrupted.

"By then I think she was seeing someone else and I was back in the frat house flipping quarters into beer glasses. Anyway, I've always regretted that I didn't pursue Libby, or at least tell her how I felt. I was never good at telling people how I felt. I wouldn't have even thought of going to her then...fear of rejection and all. Or worse, maybe I was afraid of where it would have taken me if she had been interested in pursuing our relationship."

"I can't believe you fell in love with someone you hardly knew."

Believe it or not, it was love (or the potential thereof) – not the immature imitation. Somehow, though too late, I knew that she was right for me and that every other girl I knew was not. In those days when Jimmy Carter was President young men felt a certain permission to lust after attractive women. There was plenty of that; and we might have even, on occasion, thought it was love. But it wasn't real. This was. Libby was one with whom I could spend my lifetime.

Though I don't believe that there is a perfect partner created for each of us (even if the church is to be that partner), I was certainly drawn to her and couldn't stop thinking about her. My desire was more significant than anything known to my senses, and the splendor of her character was more profound than the qualities I mentioned to Jim. Our college campus was small and every time I saw her I was struck by something, a very strong attraction at minimum.

Like a shooting star, she appeared without warning and faded fast. But the power of her presence lingered within me.

"To me, it was love. I know it." I protested his comment, wanting him to understand my feelings.

So I continued. "And I think Mary Kate sparked something similar in me." It really was similar...yet different. "The last time I had seen her and her family she was with her boyfriend and they looked so happy. So that's probably why I dreamed that I was getting robbed, LaChance. My heart, my soul, my very core, was getting broken into so I woke up to check out the 'shadow side' of myself, as Jung called it.

"You see, I sort of slept through my opportunities to really love when I was younger. I went through all the motions, but felt none of the emotions. I was so out of touch with my feelings and I regret that.

"So I'm getting re-awakened now to realize that, in some mysterious way, God is delivering me a chance to sign on to love and to be loved in ways that are too much for me to grasp."

"It's interesting," he interjected, "that you wanted to receive it, but, at the same time, it was too much to handle and it over-powered you."

"Or maybe I have to be overpowered to pay attention. Remember the hard heart and thick skull you told me about?"

That last comment brought a little smile to his face.

"When it – love – was delivered by the big guy, the mysterious one, it overtook your whole being." It seemed to me like Jim was enjoying this unraveling of my psyche or the unveiling of my soul.

"Wow, if this is only a one or two minute dream, I can't imagine what kind of complicated creatures we must be." He made his observation as though it were a totally new epiphany.

I continued my revelations while he thought about the words he just uttered. "My solution for coping with this break-in and hostile take-over was to get emergency help, to call someone on the outside to help me, someone who would treat it with importance because his or her job is to solve my problem. Kind of like Andy does."

He knew what I meant. Andy was continuously going to see counselors, psychiatrists, psychologists, and medical doctors to help him solve his life, as if life was a problem.

"But it's a kid who answers my call for help."

"That's not the response you were hoping for," Jim understated the cruelty of the little brat's insulting, mocking laughter. "Why do you think the kid laughed in your ear?"

"I think it's the child I used to be, long before college and high school, the kid who played outside and got dirty, trashed the house and didn't care too much about the results of his actions. The kid is giving me the response I need. But you're right, it's not the one I want. It's the same general response you were giving me a couple of weeks ago: laugh a little, lighten up, enjoy life more. It might be tied in with Jesus' command to not hinder the child I once was. I don't know.

"And I think it's also tied in with telling me to remember that God is love, and that whatever I think I may have been robbed of can easily be replaced. Even lost, romantic love can be replaced by a love that's more powerful than I'm able to handle. I think it's the kind of love O'Hara found in the priesthood and the kind that he wants me to take and receive, even though he knows it will be difficult and dreadful for me at times. He wants to assist in delivering it to me because, in that way, I will be more willing to take it on."

"So you don't accept my theory that this is about you remembering to alarm the house before you turn in at night?" he joked.

I wanted to tell him about the voice that instructed me to pursue my desires as a way to loving others, but sensed that it would be too much for him to focus on at that hour. Whereas earlier he looked exhilarated, now he looked exhausted.

"I accept your theory," I responded. "I just don't think it has anything to do with what I'm concerned about."

It is true. Not only did I forget to alarm the house, sometimes I forgot to lock the doors. Once I even left the front door opened all night long, not real smart in our part of town. Andy and Jim gave me hell about it.

Even though his mind was fading, LaChance wasn't finished with his line of questioning yet: "And what if a mysterious messenger comes in the middle of the night?"

I thought for a moment, then answered. "Well, if it's my dream, I hope I won't be afraid to receive what he or she is bringing to me." I emphasized "she" as though I almost anticipated receiving a message from the woman of my dreams. Did I?

We had joked periodically about how the priesthood is a wonderful way to meet wonderful women. They, like others, come to us and reveal deep truths and passionate struggles; for they come to us seeking communion with God. And, as priests, we have to remember why they come to the Church and seek our confidence. The relationship between priest and parishioner is meant to be so much more profound than human attraction. As humans, however, we know that human attractions are sometimes present.

I paused before blurting out something that I hadn't yet thought. "And I guess in my life I shouldn't be afraid of his kind of love overtaking me."

I wasn't sure if by "his kind of love" I was referring to the

141

messenger's or to God's or to Monsignor's. It is probably all the same in my mind anyway. Loyal Jim continued to listen as I continued to talk. "And I guess it can come in forms that appear to be scary and unattractive like the inner city, or even childish like..."

"...Like Mary Kate in the third grade. I can't believe she's a grown woman now!" Jim thought about his own age and realized that time is ticking.

The loquacious mouth that returned home the hour before gave in to one that struggled to form words at all, taking cues from his eyes which could no longer remain open. When he looked at his watch, he knew that he had reason to feel his tired state, for the day was over and the time had become very late on us.

LaChance went up to his room and got undressed for bed; he thought that the mystery of God must be trying to "break-in" to many people's lives.

As we former seminarians remember from our philosophy and scripture studies, there are many kinds of love, though we capture all of them in our one little, four-letter English word. How can it contain so much without bursting? Eros, philia and agape in the Greek...amor, amicitia, dilectio and caritas in the Latin – they point to many concepts: desire for what is good, friendly feelings for others, esteem, passion, communion, delight in another, and a generous giving of self. We were taught that God is love. But more than any lessons on definitions or languages, we are expected to comprehend that love is the only force more powerful than even life or death. If God is love, then the mysterious message delivered to each of us is worth receiving.

Three weeks after that late night conversation with my friend, Jim LaChance, he moved to his exurban apartment to become the pastor of an already large, and continually growing community which doesn't yet have a church building.

I guess that the Bishop has to send the priests where the people are going. Few of them are going to our inner city.

The issues out there will be incredibly different from those he dealt with for the past seven years of his life. I have no doubt, however, that those years will help him immensely as he breaks new ground with new people.

On Feeding & Anointing the Sick

7

I headed out the front door of the church's rectory to walk to a nursing home just three blocks away. The warm air of summer felt nice.

I always remove my wallet before walking in the area around the Church to dodge assailants and those who seek handouts. Word spreads quickly in inner city neighborhoods of whether or not "preachers" give away money to those who beg or if we keep any on us for those who steal.

Mass is held each Wednesday morning at the Parkway Nursing Home. I suspect that there are only two or three residents who are actually Catholics, but nearly thirty of them attend the weekly Mass. Though I don't mind leading old, dying people in prayer each week, I dislike the idea of having the Catholic Mass for people who are mostly non-Catholic, and mostly non-aware.

But it has "always been that way" so the local pastor is expected to continue the tradition. "Always" refers to a time, forty years earlier in history, when three priests lived in that rectory and worked at that Church which, in those days, went by another name. In those days, multitudes of white papists lived in the surrounding area and occupied nearly all beds of this geriatric center, too. In those days, priests had little to do but say Mass for them, and then look for other places to say Mass. In those days, that was their primary strategy for evangelization.

Even though I consider such Masses to be aberrations, and even though I don't favor this particular weekly task (the task of spewing out ritual texts to people who can't hear, or won't listen, and of distributing the Holy Eucharist to people who have no idea what it is), I do want to support the nursing home. I do want to comfort the residents. I do want to encourage the administrators. They are good neighbors who invest in the neighborhood around us. They employ many area residents. They put former welfare recipients to work, provide training for their jobs and education for promotions, advance their pay and responsibility as soon as they prove themselves worthy, even provide day care for their children and elderly relatives who cannot be left at home alone. I hope, and even pray, that my own church community will follow their lead and reinvest in the city by investing in the people who dwell among us.

A half block away from the rectory, an elderly man suddenly began to walk alongside of me. It was as though he appeared out of nowhere. At the time, it didn't occur to me how unusual it is to encounter another white pedestrian. The man, several inches shorter than me, had white hair and wore a big smile on his face. I didn't recognize him at first glance.

"How are you doing?" I asked, using the same greeting I offer most strangers I encounter.

"I'm doing grand, Tom, just grand. See, the arthritis is gone, and I'll have no trouble keeping up with you."

When I did recognize Monsignor O'Hara, I was not frightened in the least. In fact, I was almost relieved.

"I've missed you so much, Monsignor." I entered the conversation casually and eagerly as we walked on, side by side. I was glad to be in the presence of my mentor and friend once again. The time in between our encounters had grown wider. In my mind's eye I conjured up an image of Simon Peter walking along the shores of Tiberias with the resurrected Jesus.

"Tom, I've listened to you tell others of how the Wise Men received messages in a dream, and of how wise people still seek God. You'll be a modern day wise guy if you will follow your own advice. Keep with the search and trust in the revelation. Don't be afraid of the darkness. They traveled in the darkness. And don't be concerned about living among the lowly. That's where their search took them, too."

After a moment of silence, he added, "Remember what the great mystics told us: 'As you search for God, know that God searches for you even more.'"

There was so much I wanted to ask him, to tell him. Excitedly, I anticipated his responses to the eternal questions of the existence of God, the meaning of life, the purpose of suffering, the mysteries of life after death. But all that I could manage to get out of my mouth was: "I guess I am frightened sometimes by the poverty and darkness that surrounds me here."

"Some of it's out here," O'Hara gestured, lifting his hands and looking in the directions around us.

"And some of it's in here," he added as the fingers on his hands pointed to me. Then his right hand touched my chest and felt my heartbeat.

"These old people you're about to visit now," he continued, "they face a darkness, too. But many of them have, through the blessing of time, discovered what Jesus meant when He said to them: 'Fear is useless, what is needed is trust.' They bear their final crosses of old age and lingering terminal illnesses. But they're realizing that they don't have to carry their burden alone."

"But they seem so all alone," I protested. "There are so many

146

of them, all there together, and yet they each seem to be alone."

"I guess you've learned by now that if you share in the priest-hood of Christ you are destined to be an eternal companion of the misfortunate. Or is it that you are afraid that you'll grow old all alone?"

"I'm afraid that I won't know that I'm happy."

I remembered how Mary Kate had said that what each person seeks is happiness in its various forms. "You were so happy, Monsignor. Your whole priesthood was rich. And it enriched others, including the misfortunate. When you were around, I felt so alive...because you were so alive!"

"You're not poor because you don't possess many things. You're only poor if you crave more than you have. Being fully alive is a choice. If you choose it, you'll be happy," he responded.

"You once told me that we priests need to keep things in perspective, that we shouldn't complicate simple things, and that we shouldn't oversimplify things that are truly complicated. I don't know if I should be a priest any more. As I've come to know people, I've stopped respecting the Church's laws for them. I don't think I'm making any impact here. And I think I've forgotten how to love, if I ever really knew. Is this simple or complicated?"

"Oh, Tom," he cocked his head and grinned, "it's both. This struggle of yours will not be in vain. But it would be a crime if you ignored it. Your willingness to struggle will reflect your value as a priest and, more importantly, your value as a person. This moment of your longing is a time in which you can be purified so that you can go deeper into the mystery of God's love. When you go deeper you will discover gratitude. Gratitude is the door that opens to life, to the place of happiness. Don't worry about the impact you're making around here. That's God's job. Yours is to trust God and let him work through you. His own son thought the rules were a bit overdone, too."

As we approached the parking lot of the nursing home, I

147

wondered when I would see my mentor again.

"Monsignor, even my prayers seem to be dry and without meaning – both on my part and God's. It's as though the interchange is given and received in darkness."

We eased our pace as the old priest responded by continuing with his instruction.

"The mystics welcomed the darkness as the way to find the light within them. The first story of creation begins in it. The last Gospel story ends in it. But in these, and in every story in between them, light comes to dispel the darkness. Sometimes it's in extraordinary ways, like God's command: 'Let there be light,' and sometimes in ordinary ways, like Jesus' starting a fire to cook some fish on the beach for his friends one morning. It will happen in your story, too."

As we reached the main entrance of the Nursing Home, I didn't need to wonder if he was going on or stopping in for "the breaking of the bread." My mind had already been opened; my heart burned within me.

I noticed a small brown and black butterfly hovering over some shrubbery to the side of the entryway. It was not particularly beautiful, but it captured my attention. There was a spider's web formed on a corner of the canopy that I would walk under to enter the building.

"Monsignor," I asked, "do you think my search will lead me to discover the dream I'm searching for?"

The butterfly began flitting around the doorway. I hoped that it would avoid the web. It was too early in its life to meet that kind of an end.

"I don't have the answers to satisfy your eternal questions. But you do."

It was as though he read my mind.

"Your story of love is the story of God's love," he continued. "Your desire to measure how much you love the Lord will be measured by how you shepherd your flock. As you keep trying to assist in the resurrection of your community, the neighborhood and the church, other resurrections will follow. Keep your heart open and the love you want will be given and received, just as you intend your prayers to be. If God tells you to travel by another route, it doesn't mean another vocation. It means another route for this one. Pathways to glory change with time. Love will come to you, deeper and richer, but not on your conditions. The darkness will be dispelled by the light. Spread the light by serving others to the best of your ability. Remember that. It's foundational to your faith."

I walked through the front door alone. As I did, I saw the usual wheelchairs with their passengers parked in front of the big window that looked out onto the parking lot. A few of those residents who could push themselves escorted me to the dining room for our Mass. I walked beside a few of them for the additional ten yards to the room where we gather for our weekly prayer.

There were the rest of them, patiently waiting inside the large room, waiting for me like they waited for everything else – even death. There was Jasper. He had been a Buffalo Soldier in the war fifty years ago. He can still tell stories about his proud service to our country, even though he has trouble talking, and listeners have to fill in words for the ones they can't make out. And there was Bessie. She was once a dancer, but at ninety-one years old, she can't even take a step now. She is always cold and each day she appears wearing the same heavy sweater, a black shawl, and a patched blanket over her legs. And there was Thelma. She doesn't have legs anymore, but there she was in her usual chair in its usual place.

They, and others, had told me stories about growing up black in the first part of the current century. They told me about how they got scolded by priests who told them to leave the white, Catholic churches, about how they had to go to General Hospital #2 because General Hospital #1 was for whites only, about how

149

they were knocked down, cussed out, spit on, and tortured. It sounded similar to Jesus' final walk, the ultimate walk of rejection.

A tiny lady whose name I didn't know raised her arms when she heard me enter the room. She is blind now and spends most of her time praising God and being glad to be alive one more day. She throws up a few "amens" and "alleluias" during the prayers of the Mass, whenever it feels right to her.

Some of the others were in the dining hall-turned-sanctuary simply because the employees left them there from breakfast time, or because those residents prefer to be in the company of others or where any action at all is taking place.

Most of them slept through the scriptural reading that morning, as they slept through most things most mornings. Their mouths hung open and their heads drooped. A few of them offered a prayer when I asked what they would like to say to God. Usually one or two of them dominate the prayers.

I led them in a few songs, as I do each week, always the same ones – the only ones to which I know a complete verse. I responded to a question after someone addressed it to me during the Eucharistic Prayer and then repeated it in a shouting tone. The seniors put up with one another every day of the week, so I have resolved to put up with their distractions for the half hour, or so, that I am with them.

When I elevated the bread and the wine, which I believe had become the body and blood of Christ, one lady yelled out, "Who was that you were talkin' to outside?"

I stopped and looked at her. Though I realize that many of the residents are in and out of reality, conditioned by their old minds and new drugs, I wondered what she saw. I wanted so badly to hear from her vantagepoint of much wisdom, much imagination or much senility. After the Mass I would ask her to tell me about the scene in the parking lot that she had witnessed, even though I was certain that her response would be on some unrelated topic by that time.

During communion, I broke off a tiny piece of the wafer for each of those who were alert enough to receive it. I reached out and gave a blessing to those who were not.

I thought it odd that, throughout the years in which I had been saying Mass at this geriatric center, none of these old people died. The same people were in the room for this most recent Mass who were there when I said my first Mass at the Parkway Nursing Home nearly five years earlier.

I called for an employee's assistance when one lady began to cough, choke, and then spit. Though it seemed to me that she might be dying, no one else seemed to notice, or care. No one reacted to the situation but me, not even the health care worker who passed through the dining room at that precise moment.

The holy Mass wasn't unfolding in the way it was intended. After she spit out what was in her mouth, I knelt down before her and picked up the tiny particle of bread from her saliva. That is the Bread of Life! It is given to heal her, to save her, to set her free from her confinement. How could it be spewed from her being? Why was there such disorder to this sublime event?

Humans hunger for perfection and humans thirst for God. But my world is so imperfect. God keeps offering me, and those around me, the gruesome realities of human conditions which keep us from perfection and also keep many of us from God.

Another woman rolled herself over to the place where I knelt and seized my arm as she found me on her level in front of the gagging woman. I looked at her and asked her what was wrong. But she didn't speak. I wasn't sure that I had ever heard her speak. We had never communicated before, except when I reached out to give the tiny wafer each week, or reached out to touch her hand occasionally when saying "hello" or "good-bye." She has deep-set eyes that stared at me as though she could see right

through me. I felt captured; my arm was in her grab. I gazed
back wanting to know what she could see inside of me.

But the moment was broken by another woman who, from
the back of the room, yelled out, "Bring me some juice! Father,
let us drink the juice today!"

I panned my eyes over the crowd. Some slept on, with their
heads bowed down, some stared straight ahead, some mumbled
words or hummed tunes, not realizing that they were doing so.
The scene looked like what I imagined formless chaos to be. I
wondered if, by any chance, the Holy Spirit hovers above this
sight. I wanted to know what kind of sacred life could rise from
this weekly last supper with these forgotten disciples.

To the woman who reached out to me, I wanted to reach back.
Before leaving, I reached instead for my holy oils and anointed
her head and hands: "...May the Lord in his love and mercy help
you...May God who forgives all sins save you..."

Whether or not she asked for, or appreciated, this sacrament
or even knew what it meant, I did. Like a lot of people around
me, I sometimes lack faith and I sometimes lack love. But God
help me if I ever lack hope.

When I left the building, there was a light rain falling down
from somewhere above. I buried the fragment of heavenly host
in the earth near where the butterfly had earlier flown and landed.
But it was gone now. I cannot fathom how Jesus could love the
unlovable so much that he would die for us.

As I walked back to the Church, I thought about some of the
messages that Monsignor had delivered to me. "Love will come
...but not on your conditions...being alive is a choice...you're only
poor if you crave more than you have...as you search for God,
know that God searches for you even more."

BOOK 3

Wild Grapes

"The joy and hope, the grief and anguish of the men of our time, especially of those who are poor or afflicted in any way, are the joy and hope, the grief and anguish of the followers of Christ as well."

– Vatican II, Gaudium et Spes

On Eucharist: Blood Poured Out

1

As I stood before the congregation on Sunday, I knew that we had not had a good week.

Two days earlier at a bus stop a few blocks away from our church, a sixth grader got a gun shoved into his gut by two teenagers wearing ski masks. One held the gun, while the other unfastened the gold-plated chain that the young boy was wearing around his neck. There were two other teenagers in the car, which slowed down to let them out. When they had completed their robbery of the child, it sped away with the perpetrators who jumped back into the car's right side seats. The middle school student was in church that Sunday morning and listened as I recounted his ordeal to all who gathered.

The night before that Friday, a lady in the neighborhood received a fire-bomb through the front window of her house. She is an activist who has continually denounced the drug dealers who make a living on her block; she is also known to call the police when the dealing gets out of hand. The damaging ball of

159

fire arrived in the middle of the night, but the explosion woke her in time to extinguish the flames before much destruction occurred.

And a couple of days before that, there had been a shoot-out across the street from our church on Spartan Parkway. Three boys shot each other up when their drug deal went sour. Each of the three carried a gun. Each of the three suffered the impact of at least one bullet. Two of them will be physically okay, but the third will probably be paralyzed for the rest of his life. A couple of their relatives, members of the church, were present to catch this sermon, too.

My own personal encounter with trouble helped me to identify with those who were victimized during the week. During the Mass, I made reference to a kid down the street who yelled all kinds of obscenities at me, expletives that I chose not to repeat – not because we were in church, but because repeating them would serve no purpose except entertainment for some listeners. I told them, though, that the kid threatened to kill me if I didn't get out of his neighborhood.

"I'm gonna kill ya if ya don't get da hell outta here," the boy warned me.

Many of those in the congregation knew that I was referring to D.L., a young neighborhood punk. D.L. talks to priests in the same manner in which he talks to anyone else who gets in his way – including the mayor himself. If he didn't like someone, he simply didn't like him (or her). But he probably wouldn't talk that way to the police chief. He was always in some trouble, but never in big trouble; he was savvy enough to stay out of big trouble.

I had read for the assembly several verses from the twenty-first chapter of *The Holy Gospel According to Matthew* about a story that Jesus once told his followers. It was about a vineyard and some crazy tenant farmers who raised wild grapes in it.

"...The vineyard owner got upset, naturally, and he sent his servants to straighten out the problem...two groups, two times."

I attempted to explain some of the meanings behind the passage as well as some of its relevance for our faith community.

"But the servants got badgered and abused by the unruly tenants. So then he sent his own son, thinking that the son would represent his authority to them – his power and his glory. But they killed his son. So, in his anger, the father-owner got rid of those wicked tenant farmers and replaced them with new ones who could yield a bountiful harvest for a crop of good wine.

"...God entrusted the Jewish nation, his chosen people, with the harvest of humanity in the Old Testament. He commissioned the Christian community, his adopted children, with the same task in the New Testament. Both religious groups came up short. Prophets and teachers have been sent through the ages to straighten us out. But we've done everything from ignore them to martyr them.

"And now we are writing a third testament by the lives we live in these vineyards of our habitat, the vineyards which surround us and surround our church. To me, the grapes are still wild, the crop is still sour, the blood is still being poured out. And it's spoiling the soil in which we are raising up the next generation, the next crop."

I thought that my preaching was making an impact. I wanted to offer something that would help Sunday last into Monday and then remain relevant for the rest of the week. I wanted to make sure that those who gathered understood my correlation between the vineyards and the streets.

"We've got a lot of work to do in this vineyard we are tending," I told them. "I'm tired of this culture of violence that stares us down when we walk outside, that frightens our elders and frightens our babies, that rips at our homes and rips at our hearts. I'm sick of the handgun laws that have shot holes in our value systems and have forced all of us to attend far too many funerals of children we know and of friends who shouldn't have had to die. I've had enough of the example we, adults, have been setting, by drinking and drugging, then driving and losing control. That's no way to raise up a good crop. It'll only plow them down. And I don't want to have to counsel even one more spouse who comes to me because domestic violence has beat her up again, and victimized the entire household beyond repair again, only to allow the family perpetrator back into the home again, until it happens the next time...and the next time...and the next time.

"I have been sent to this vineyard. Today it looks to me like a vineyard of abuse, addiction, and adultery, a vineyard of gangs, guns, and gambling with human lives. I see the wild grapes. I smell the sour grapes. And I beg you to help me cultivate and nurture a rich harvest here."

Before I sat down, I threw one more punch. I aimed it at some of the adults in our parish who are continuously fighting with one another about unimportant things. I didn't say their names, but I didn't have to. Most everyone recognized which direction my words were being sent.

There is one particular man who told people not to trust the priest – not just me, in particular, but any priest. He demanded that I give him a personal account of all the money that comes into the church and all the money that goes out from it. He remained unconvinced after I told him that our financial records are open to all interested parties. He referred to me as "the plantation owner" and said that he "wouldn't be no 'Uncle Tom'" to me. Unfortunately, that man was elected as a Parish Council officer, a leader among the people. I suppose that apathy among the masses is to blame.

In addition, there are two women who constantly fight each other and pressure other women to choose sides. One is the president of the Altar Society. The other is the president of the Women's Club. Their two church groups are like two street gangs. The "crips" and the "bloods" might be tougher on the outside, but these gangs are every bit as mean. Though I suspect they are probably harmless to each other, they are certainly a nuisance to the community and to me.

Others like Ms. Bodreaux just talk on the phone most days drumming up some news, making up some gossip to fill in the blanks for details that she (and they) do not know as bona fide hearsay. I was tired of their behavior, too. So I addressed it from the pulpit that Sunday morning.

"How are we ever going to raise up a rich harvest with these attitudes?" I asked them. "How are we ever going to pass along hope to the next generation with these behaviors? If you want to get mad at other people or get mad at issues, let me give you some issues worth getting mad about. Let me give you some people who you can focus your anger upon. Let's stop gossiping about, and mistrusting, those who are trying to build the kingdom of God, and let's go after those who are trying to tear it down.

"Get mad at the drug dealers who are killing our children. Get mad at the legislators who are handing out guns to the gangs. Get mad at those among us who ignore these problems, thereby allowing them to perpetuate, increase, and overtake us like wild grapes overtaking a potentially healthy vineyard."

The people didn't seem to comprehend what I intended by my words. They heard but they didn't listen. Sometimes I wonder if it makes any sense for me to talk if no one listens. It often seems that they don't grasp my intent, at least not enough to want to change the ways in which they put their faith into action. Some of them even tell me that I don't get through, don't connect.

"Fatha you want us to go out and change the neighborhood," Ms. Bodreaux told me in the heavy accent from her native Louisiana roots. "But we come inside the walls of this church on Sundays so's we can get away from all the neighborhood out there. Don't you understand that?"

"I understand that this church is an oasis of hope for you," I replied. "But I don't think the oasis has to be limited to just this one day or just this one spot. I want to help you turn our entire surroundings into a place of hope!"

"Well I don't know how you're gonna do that," she said as she walked away from me.

I struck out with her again.

She especially frustrates me because she rarely looks up during the Mass. To do so would disturb her rosary that she dutifully recites to herself during our time of communal prayer. In the hour and a half that it takes to say the Sunday "Gospel Mass," she can say all five decades of all three mysteries, do a novena, and still find time to follow part of the Mass prayers in the handy little missalette.

Many moments of many prayers of mine are spent wishing that I could enter into her mind, and into those belonging to others like her, to discover a way to make them understand how their lives could be enriched. I want so badly to show them how they can put their valuable faith into practical action.

The man who I referred to before as the parish leader who doesn't trust priests came up to me after Mass one Sunday and said, "we don't want you white priests serving us black folks anymore."

I surprised even myself with my calm response.

"If that's what you want, then please help me to call black seminarians forth from our community so that they can serve as priests. Please!"

"They won't come forth with your crazy rules for them," he replied. "Call them yourself."

"How can I respond to that?" I wondered out loud. But the man had already walked away.

It sometimes seems that everywhere I turn I am shown more inconsistencies and contrasts – many that are blatant. As this particular church leader walked away, I found myself becoming angry at all the wicked people who wouldn't think of missing Mass on Sunday mornings because it would be "sinful" to do so. I desired to possess the attitude of those who stayed away from churches on Sunday mornings, who refused to confuse religion with spirituality, who were appalled by the hypocrisy of organized religions.

Attempting to make the most of where I found myself (in front of a congregation assembled to hear about God), I delivered my sermon about our vineyard. Then I instructed the teenagers who were present to stand up and step into the middle aisle of the church. I wanted to demonstrate the importance of unifying faith and praxis.

Somewhere near the back of the church a young man named Talib reached over and hit his brother on the chest with the back of his hand saying, "Okay, Vincent, here we go again."

They looked at each other knowing that this wasn't the first time that I had done something like what I was doing at that moment. I urged the adults to know the youth and, if they didn't, I urged them to learn something about the next generation by taking an interest in one or more of them...and thereby learn about their potential...and thereby learn about the kind of future they each want.

There were about twenty teens standing in the middle of the church for the adults to look over. Some are older than Vincent's seventeen years, but most are younger. He and his brother are the tallest ones, though. The two of them had responded to a request that I recently made of them to serve as role models and mentors for the younger teenagers. And they did fine. They told me that "the guys are okay, but the girls have too many issues." Though it was difficult for them to assume leadership status among the other kids, they did a good job.

Vincent is starting his senior year of high school. Ever since Sister Mary Ellen and I took an interest in him and Talib, they liked doing things for the church. Though they couldn't motivate the rest of their family to go to church with them very often, the two of them are present nearly every Sunday. During the recent summers, Sister Mary Ellen and I provided one (or in the case of last summer, both) of them with a job at our church cutting grass, packing shelves in the food pantry, keeping the grounds and surrounding neighborhood picked up, and organizing events for our youth group. Last summer we acquired enough grant money to include Talib, too.

They are not really brothers. In the African-American system, as I have come to understand it, you're suppose to have the same mother if you want to say that somebody is really your brother or your sister. Talib and Vincent don't have the same mother or the same father, but they do have a family now, headed by Talib's mom and Vincent's dad.

Vincent hardly remembers his real mother. But he remembers enough to have strong feelings about her. When he was five years old, she decided that she didn't want him anymore. So she called his dad and told him to come and get the boy. His dad already had another family by then, but he was happy to take Vincent in to live with them. He wanted his first child from the beginning. I don't know what happened to make his real mom want to give him away the way she did, or at the time she did. But Vincent has never seen her since and, as he told me, "I don't want to see her ever again."

His mom, now, is the mother of Talib as well as the mother of Jeannetta and Vonell and Rasheena, who recently turned two years old. Talib is a little more than one year younger than Vincent, but he's already taller. There is an obvious competition between them. Vincent is a slightly better athlete and he gets better grades in school, but Talib is better at computer games and often beats his older brother at one-on-one hoops. They are also best friends. Vincent is much shyer than Talib. The younger brother talks constantly and usually doesn't know when to keep quiet. He was poking at Vincent's back as he stood behind his older brother in our church's center aisle.

"Look at that girl over there," Talib must have repeated it

166

three times. His words rattled out of his mouth in a rapid, excited fashion. He was pointing at a young girl who looked back at them. She was still sitting, even though I instructed the teenagers to stand. Vincent had noticed her at church once before. I think she sometimes visits her church-going grandmother on weekends. The girl is good-looking and that's why Talib was poking his brother and whispering so loud.

I was still talking to the adults. I asked all the men who are fathers of these children to stand up. Only three men stood. We applauded those three who were present with their children. Then I said: "If there is any other man present who is willing to be available for these young people as a mentor and role-model, I want you to stand up and be noticed by this community."

It seemed like about fifty men stood. I asked those fifty to walk into the center aisle on either side of the teens. Then I asked each man to put a hand on one of the young shoulders as a sign that they would be present to the young person who they reached out and touched. It would serve as a sign that they would help the young person to shoulder the responsibilities of the tough choices they have to make.

After that, some of the women stood, too, as a sign that they would work in the vineyard also, to create a better existence for our youth. The women don't get as much attention from me as the men do because, as I told the ladies many times: "I know you'll be there – you've always been the backbone of the family and the backbone of the church."

Most of the teenagers don't mind the people in church staring at them and making them the center of attention for a little while. But the kids know it won't last. Because it hasn't in the past. They anticipated that after the Mass the adults would fight over something else, something totally without merit. They are worse than little kids. But Sister Mary Ellen and I really do try to motivate them to live better, more spiritual, lives.

It concerns me that they watch each other come to the altar

167

for holy communion, then make comments to their groupies like: "Why did he go up – he's divorced," or "did you see her popping her gum – doesn't care what she's receivin' on top of it."

I tried to teach them that all of us who are called forward by Jesus are a collection of sinners as much as we are a communion of saints. We are not here to judge what's in the hearts of others. Our weekly trip to the altar is a process of approaching, requesting, accepting, acknowledging, taking, receiving, tasting, swallowing, consuming, and becoming. It is the process of becoming the Christ we receive.

I'm not sure that they agree.

So, at each Mass I drink from my cup of salvation and hope that it means something.

Vincent's Hope and Confirmation

2

"You've got to be patient with these people, Thomas," my remarkable pastoral associate, Sister Mary Ellen, told me many times. "They don't have very much power or control in their lives...not in their public schools, not in their city government, usually not at their jobs, often not even in their homes. They're living in houses they don't own – they are homes where someone else makes the rules. But at church, they get to have a little power. They experiment with it, play around with it. And they'll make some mistakes with it, and even abuse their power sometimes. But they need to be shown how to handle it. You and I need to encourage them, and forgive them, and then welcome them back and encourage them some more."

She is sympathetic to me, but also challenges me to grow in pastoral leadership.

"I know it's difficult for you, Thomas. When everybody struggles for power, fights are bound to occur. But how else are they going to learn unless we provide them a loving environment in which they can do so?"

She and I truly believe that if a church doesn't make a real difference in a neighborhood, then that church has no business existing in that neighborhood. But we also realize that if we are ever going to help create a good environment out there, we will have to start by creating one in here – in the church, in our works, and in our hearts.

This third and final part of my story considers the people of God, the church. Certainly this ecclesial institution of ours is made up of all kinds. Some of us are a bit wacky. Some are incredibly Christ-like. Each of us has been shaped by this humanly divine vessel. It teaches us, shaped by the issues and personalities that guide us.

Some who read my tale may wonder why I've bothered with this third book, a story partly about church politics, man-made laws. It's probably not as intriguing or important as some of the outer works by which the church manifests itself and some of the inner struggles through which its laborers journey.

My point of telling it is simple. The church, though ever good are its intentions, has overpowered many Catholics through the years like a monster. Before its strength, they kneel and cower in the dark corners of its abandoned sanctuaries, dimly lit with the flicker of flames that try to enlighten us with some good news.

In spite of the many tiers of membership in our Church, I contend that we can work as one body. It would be nice if we became the perfect Body of Christ, but we won't – we're noticeably imperfect, wrought with arrogance and guilt and misunderstanding and hurt. But we're no monster.

Yet in counseling parishioners, I know that's how many perceive us. Their faith journeys seem not unlike the social and physical journey of an innocent child who, when beginning to blossom, has something horrible happen to her. A monster overpowers her, hurts her, strips her of dignity and hope, while watching her bring upon herself guilt, shame, anger and even despair. Shaped by experiences and history, the aberrations of both the dark ages and the modern age, the Church has overpowered – seemingly raped – many innocent souls full of potential and hope. My constant plea to those who have been hurt is that we're not the monster. I cannot usually convince them.

My purpose of writing this third offering is to suggest that if we work together – pastors and parishioners, the satisfied and the dissatisfied, the powerful and the powerless – we can keep the flame of faith burning. We can even spread the flicker of hope to the darkest dregs of society where the warmth and brilliance of the sun of God might actually shine. Our earthly Body of Christ will continue imperfect and unjust. But I am certain that we can tame the threat of monsters when we articulate our fears as well as our dreams, just as I do with my friend Jim, realizing that they lose their power over me once I talk about them.

But the true test will be with our young people when they discover what it is that we have handed on to them. What are we giving them?

In our city, we have already taken away their neighborhood schools, bussing them across town to places they don't care to go, to be among people who don't care to have them. Our neighborhoods have suffered greatly, for children aren't receiving a healthy sense of neighboring. In our inner city, we have taken away their churches and parochial schools, consolidating them by twos and threes, only to close them one by one.

Saint Peter Claver Church is made up mostly of people who sought religious sanctuary after the doors of their own churches were closed and those buildings were sold. In our society, we have even taken away their families, accepting as normal – divorce, institutional child-care and nursing homes, as well as other temporary or permanent breaks to family life. What are we contributing to our young people's tomorrow? How does the Church provide a model for them to follow? Or is traditional Catholi-

171

cism like traditional business and industry, incapable of functioning according to contemporary needs? Does my job of giving away food and praying at funerals make a difference to those around me? These are the issues I raise in this third book.

The church is forming Vincent like so many other young people. One of the reasons that I took an interest in him is because I like the choices that he made. And I told him so. He came to see me for the first time a few years ago, before I knew who he was. During that conversation, I asked him what it is like to be a young teenager, living where he lives, facing the daily difficulties he faces. I was still relatively new to the area then.

"Father, some of my friends tell me that, growing up in the ghetto, I've got to make a choice: sell drugs or stay poor," he said. "But Father, I don't think those are my only choices."

"What are your choices, Vincent?"

I was very curious, interested in understanding the mind of a young man reared in poverty, even though I realized I never could truly understand.

He revealed to me his constant dilemma.

"Like most of the guys out there, I know that if I work hard at McDonald's after school and on weekends, I can make up to two hundred dollars in one week. And I know that if I deal drugs, I can make up to two grand in one day. What do you think we should choose, Father?"

"It depends on what you want. Why did you choose McDonald's?"

"Because I know what I don't want. I've seen too many guys get busted and messed up. I don't want to spend my time in jail or doped up. I want to be an aeronautic engineer. I don't mind flipping hamburgers for a while. I've got to keep my sights set on what's down the road though. Those other guys don't believe there's a tomorrow..."

"...And you do." I finished the sentence for him.

172

"I sure want to," he responded, not sure if I was making a statement or asking a question. Then he thought, "I wish my brother wanted to believe it also."

When his younger brother was fourteen, he got tangled up with a group that smoked crack. They dipped it in embalming fluid for kicks. That combination was supposed to make them feel incredibly good. When Vincent found out, he told Talib how stupid it is, how much trouble it could bring him, "not to mention the pain and suffering it will bring dad and mom." But the older boy really tore into Talib when he found out that the younger sibling had done some dealing out to little kids for his group of middle school hoods, who were actually selling it for one of their older brother's gang. It was a crazy cycle, typical of many crazy cycles that exist in poverty stricken areas, and Vincent helped his brother get out of it before it got to be too late for him.

"Sometimes he's pretty stupid and doesn't know the right choices to make," Vincent shared with me.

"I guess that's why you were sent to be his brother," I told him.

My friend, Mr. Simons, once told me something that I thought about when I considered these boys. He said, "I used to hang with a wild bunch 'til one day, out in the streets, I met Jesus. Everybody will run into Jesus some day. But sometimes we've got to do the introductions."

Interested in Vincent's desire to stay straight, I told him that I wanted to talk more about his plans. The next week I went to his house to talk with his dad. I told him that I was impressed with Vincent and thought that we could get some grant money from a community agency or another Catholic Church in a wealthier area to offer him a full-time summer job helping Sister Mary Ellen and me. I also wanted Vincent to help us develop a youth group for kids in the church and the neighborhood.

We never really did get a legitimate youth group going, though we began to lay the groundwork during that summer. Vincent and his brother and some of their friends got together at the church regularly. Sometimes we would rent a movie for them, then we'd discuss it. Sometimes we would set up hoops in the parking lot and they'd invite others in our neighborhood to play some ball.

They even invited some of the gang-bangers from down the street, but they didn't want to come to a church. That's okay – both that they were invited and that they refused the invitation. At least this way, they know that we reached out and that we aren't afraid.

Sister had the youth do some service projects like working in the food pantry and delivering groceries to some of the elderly citizens who can't get out anymore. Sister and I encourage them to read certain articles about faith and about decision-making that we find to be intriguing. We encourage them to develop their computer skills, to teach the younger kids in Sunday school and to organize some neighborhood clean-ups. Vincent is good at coordinating these efforts and at motivating his peers.

He likes being around the church. He told me that it beat being cramped in the smoky kitchen at McDonald's. When he asked me several months into the first summer why I had given him the job, I told him that it was because he looked right in my eyes when he talked and because he gave me a firm handshake when he introduced himself.

Vincent's response was "I guess that little things can make a difference for no apparent reason."

Since that day, he commented to me that "I know it irks you if people won't look at you when they're speaking to you."

He is probably right.

Sister Mary Ellen likes having the two boys around because it is such good encouragement for the younger children. The little ones naturally watch them and follow their lead. The hope of the church rests on these young people. Their future will be determined by their education getting united with their values.

In talking to our Youth Group once, Sister said, "While grow-

174

ing up, it is essential that you develop your spiritual side, just like you develop your physical side and your social side and your cultural side. If we are going to have a vibrant city and a vibrant church, it will be because you want one. You each have every right to become very successful and very faithful down the road. And we want you to have every opportunity, as well. We can help you if you're willing to be educated.

"But," she continued, "as much as we need smart people... more than that, we need good people."

The kids think that she is great at telling them about God and about giving them reasons why they should want to be good. Vincent told me that he is very grateful for Sister Mary Ellen and me for our interest in them. Saint John of the Cross once wrote that "gratitude is the first face of faith." It is easy to take an interest in him because of his attitude. His response and attitude also give me more hope for his peers.

But he is still a teenager. I am glad that he feels comfortable enough with us to say what is on his mind in our presence.

"With all that's going on in the world," he told me, "I sometimes think it's almost impossible to believe in God. But I know it's possible to believe in people who tell us about God. I'm glad that's what Sister and you do. Society is telling us about everything but God."

Vincent and I have had many good discussions. I admire his perspective on life and realize that I can learn much from him. He often asks me about the mystery of God, and he seems content to contemplate that mystery. Unlike me, he doesn't mind that he cannot comprehend it all. He isn't interested in grasping it. He is interested in enjoying that which he realizes he cannot comprehend. I think that his is true faith, real trust.

The Table of Our Priestly Service

3

Vincent determined that maybe I don't believe in God, based on something that he thought he heard me say one night. Regardless of what I believe about God, I hope that my young friend knows that I believe in what I am doing at St. Peter Claver Church.

About a month after my sermon on the grapes, sometime around Halloween, we hosted an important Reconciliation Service at our church. Six other priests joined us to hear people's confessions. Reconciliation services occur during Advent and Lent in most Catholic churches, but in our church they occur whenever we determine that we need them to occur. One was occurring in late October because of the old ladies in the Altar Society and the Women's Club. One of the two I told you about burst into my office one day, interrupting a counseling session to tell me that the other one had tried to kill her, or something as melodramatic as that.

Sister Mary Ellen and I work hard to convince people to talk to one another in order to settle conflicts on their own, but it

176

wasn't happening. So we decided to call God into the process of reconciliation. Sister volunteered to lead the prayers for healing at the service. And she asked me to recruit some other priests to be present to help our congregation come back to the Lord by individually confessing sins and communally pledging to build a community for God out of who we are, warts and all.

Before the service started, Sister and I hosted a dinner meeting in the St. Peter Claver Rectory. Everyone associated with this church calls our parish's office building "the rectory," even though nobody lives in it.

I asked Vincent and his brother to serve the meal, and they brought their friend DeRon along to help them. DeRon is another youth of the parish who was looking to accomplish some service hours for his Confirmation class requirement. He was disappointed to learn that serving dinner to priests wouldn't count – it isn't real service. He'd have to do something for somebody who truly depended on his help. Vincent commented that we must be doing something right if DeRon wanted service hours more than money.

Talib and his older brother knew "Father Lucca" from school, and the younger brother was nervous about serving him because he had the teacher for one of his classes.

The brothers thought that he was a good guy, even though "he acts gay." They determined that the Church must have adopted the same "don't ask – don't tell" policy that is used by our military. But it doesn't matter to them. Everybody gets along with Fr. Lucca and goes to him with their problems. And the students think it's great that he always blesses everyone, trying to make them feel good.

One of the priests who joined us that evening lives in Central America. He is actually from the Kansas City area, but just visiting his family and friends for a vacation from his church in Central America. His name is Fr. Francis Hand, but everyone calls him "Frank." He told the boys to call him Frank, too.

"Yes, sir," they responded, even though "it didn't sound proper" to them. Their mother instructed them to always show respect to all adults, especially to priests and nuns.

Frank is nearing his sixtieth birthday, but he looks older. His skin is dark and wrinkled. His hair is long and uncombed. It matches his beard. He wore an old T-shirt and khaki pants with his suede sandals.

Another priest present, dressed in black from his collar down to his shiny shoes, works at the Chancery. When the brothers arrived with DeRon at a quarter till six, I invited them to come into the room where we were meeting and say "hello" to all the guests. There were eight of us including the two who they knew: Andy and Sister Mary Ellen. I introduced the priest in black first.

When I presented him, I said, "This is Father Hubert Marshall – he is the Bishop's right hand man." Father Marshall performs his job well. He is the highest-ranking church official in our Diocese, next to the Bishop. Marshall wants to succeed and wants others to help him do so. He would like to become a bishop himself, and he'd make a good one. John Henry Newman, the nineteenth century British churchman who was eventually named to the College of Cardinals, once suggested that most priests decide early on whether they want to remain priests or become bishops, whether they want to serve others or play politics. One of the ironies, even beauties of our church's inner-workings, however, is that many who want to be bishops and play politics are never asked, while many who want to serve as priests get elevated to the episcopacy instead. I suspect that the latter group is better at leading because they're better at serving.

The three teenagers said hello and sort of bowed, thinking that he must be rather important. But actually, that introduction didn't mean a thing to them since they don't know what the Bishop has to do with any of it anyway.

An African-American priest, Fr. John Hillard, was there as

well as Jim LaChance who the boys know as the priest from the church next to their own. They also recognized the other religious sister because she lives at the convent with Sister Mary Ellen and works at the grade school. That nun is Sister Raphael.

The reason we were having the dinner meeting before the Reconciliation Service is because of Fr. Marshall and Jim who walked in together promptly at five o'clock. They wanted to discuss the Church's presence in the inner city with these other church workers who accepted our invitation to meet, as well as to stay and help with the prayer afterward.

There are only three Catholic churches left in our inner city, three food pantries, a grade school, a high school, and several programs for the elderly and the single-female-heads-of-household. Jim, Andy and I and the two nuns present are responsible for, or strongly connected with, all of these programs, institutions and ministries.

We all knew, or at least suspected, that Jim LaChance was getting transferred sometime during the year ahead. He serves as the pastor for two of the three churches. He and I, along with Sister Raphael, are in charge of the grade school. Andy is the church's liaison to the high school.

Jim asked Fr. Marshall to meet with this group so that, together, we could devise a plan for these places and services so that they would continue operating smoothly after he was gone. By 5:15, we were all sitting in the living room discussing our issue. The cook, a lady from one of Jim's parishes, was in the kitchen and the boys would soon be on their way to assist her. They know that if they walk to the church, they can always get a ride home after dark.

Marshall, the Vicar General for the Diocese, began.

"We intended to permit Jim to remain here in the Central City until next summer or autumn, but that arrangement is no longer one with which we can abide. The new community already contains over three hundred committed families. We project that

that number will double in the next three to five months. It will double again to over one thousand households in the next year. The developers are producing rapidly and the priests of the surrounding parishes do not want, or need, any supplemental duties."

The Vicar was referring to a region east of the city's suburban area, down by the Missouri River. Mansions are going up next to long standing bungalows and river shanties. Father Marshall had informed Jim that he was to go as the first pastor of the fledgling church to which his opening remarks referred. Jim would help form a new community from among those pioneers and eventually construct a new church building with them on some property that the Diocese has owned for about twenty five years, holding on to it in anticipation of growth in that direction. Recently, the three hundred families to whom Fr. Marshall referred began gathering for Sunday Masses at a new elementary school building. One of the priests from one of the churches closest to that area says the new community's one weekly Mass on Sunday afternoons.

The Vicar continued, "As you are well aware, the priest-to-people ratio is more favorable here in the Central City than in virtually any other section of our Diocese. We do not possess another presbyter to circulate here to replace Jim. He requested that, before he is transferred from this deanery, we discuss how to best discharge services to the people who reside here given the reality of one less priest."

Marshall sat up straight in his chair as though he didn't want to wrinkle his suit. He always wore a black suit when on official church business. His shirts, usually white cotton or sometimes light-colored blues or yellows, are always starched even though they are hidden by his rabat. The little hair that he has on his head was neatly arranged. He spoke in a deliberate fashion. He doesn't use contractions in his sentences and rarely uses simple words and phrases when he can avoid them.

180

No one was surprised by the Vicar's announcement. Jim had warned us that it would be coming, and he and I forewarned each of our guests when we invited them to the dinner and prayer service.

Sister Raphael responded to Fr. Marshall first.

"We all know that a significant percentage of the families who send their children to our schools don't live nearby. But they used to. They want their children to have both an Afrocentric experience and a Catholic education that teaches values and prayers. And many of those who worship in these churches don't live here, either. Maybe they should be worshipping closer to their homes and maybe they should be sending their children to schools nearer to them. But they care about this part of town and don't want us to give up on it. I hear that a lot. They are grateful that we have remained when others, businesses, and industry have gone."

She spoke in a matter-of-fact tone, though it was obvious that she holds deep personal convictions about the church's obligation to remain in the inner city. Sister Raphael came from a large, close-knit family. Though she grew up among wealth, she spent most of her years as a nun working in economically deprived areas. She is forty-six years old, thin and attractive. She wore a navy suit decorated with a small silver crucifix on its lapel. She looked fashionable as she took off her jacket, revealing a silk pastel blouse.

I tagged my own concern for our ministries onto hers.

"While LaChance is out building where everyone else is building, how do we build something worthwhile around here where it seems that things are, for the most part, getting torn down? Sister Mary Ellen is going to speak to our parishioners this evening about how Christianity means building the city of love. Having one less priest in this area seems to give the opposite message: that we can't build it here, so we've got to find it somewhere else."

Father Marshall spoke again: "We are all in this collectively and believe me, I realize that this enterprise into which we are embarking is not facile. As Frank can verify, there are localities in Latin America where the ratio between Roman Catholics and presbyters is forty-four or forty-five thousand to one. The United States and Europe have nearly seventy five percent of the world's priests. We are accustomed to having matters a certain way and we must modify our thinking so that we can assist others in altering their thinking accordingly. But I must maintain the responsibility of commissioning presbyters to where they are most needed. Would you have me embark upon this task in another manner?"

"No, of course not." Sister Mary Ellen responded to the Vicar. "I appreciate you and Jim wanting to talk this over with us. And I think I can speak for all of us when I add that we are grateful for your concern for our continued ministry in the urban core. All of us want to enhance the work of the church and offer our people hope. But given the current realities of fewer priests and religious women, the question really is: 'how do we best do what we've got to do?'"

"Well, I recommend," the Vicar started, "that Thomas assume the pastoral duties at one of Jim's parishes and that Andy reduce his academic schedule so that he can manage the helm of the other. Then I suggest we discern some practical approaches for you and Raphael to portion out appropriate administrative, sacramental, and pastoral tasks if you would be agreeable to assuming more duties than you are currently undertaking while departing to others – the laity – a portion of your current obligations."

Sister's facial response indicated to Fr. Marshall that he had replied well to her question.

Then he added, "We considered that perhaps John and Frank could offer us assistance as we advance this process."

Father John Hillard grew up in a parish near these three, but it had closed and was sold over ten years ago. He is of medium height and stocky. I was told that he was an amateur boxer be-

182

fore he entered the seminary. Older priests recall that he was rather cocky as a seminarian and expected special treatment from his superiors. If that was true, it is no longer, for he has changed with time and responsibility. He is certainly respected now as both a competent administrator and humble leader. As a black Catholic and church official, he has an obvious interest in the decisions that get made concerning the inner city. The Bishop sometimes asks for his advice, though he also respects John's wish to not be "type cast" and sent to the inner city based solely on the fact that that is where he grew up.

"Because I don't work here," Father John began, "I don't want to suggest what is best for your future. But know that I'm willing to help you determine what's best. As you know, these are my people and, even though some of them think that I've betrayed them and abandoned them, I care very much about what happens to their churches. I'm just glad we're not threatening to close any more of them."

Jim thanked John for making the effort to be present and express his support. Then he offered an invitation to the other guest. "And we're also fortunate that Frank is visiting K.C. these weeks, but sorry that we are mixing his pleasure with our business."

Then he turned to the Central American pastor. "What would they do where you live?"

Where Frank lives and works is in a small village in El Salvador about thirty miles away from the big city, San Salvador. He is actually responsible for the pastoral needs of seven or eight villages, some that he gets to visit no more than five times a year.

"We have a unique way of dealing with our problems," Frank commented with a grin. "We address them."

He was making a sarcastic reference to the ways in which he thinks that the Roman Catholic hierarchy usually deal with problems: ignore them.

"We try to match up our needs with our talents. If somebody in our community is a good teacher, for example, we ask him to teach in the church. If somebody is a good administrator, we ask her to administrate in the church. If people are good preachers, we ask them to preach. By virtue of Baptism, we are all priestly people; we all share in the priesthood of Christ. We call forth the gifts of each member to serve the needs of the others, as priests. I think you can keep, even strengthen, your ministries with one less priest...if you want to."

"How can you do that – invite others to do what people depend on priests to do? Doesn't Rome get upset?" Sister Raphael asked, looking more at Fr. Marshall than at Frank.

"As the renowned theologian, Avery Dulles, once noted, 'The responsibility of the Roman Church is two-fold,'" Marshall explained. "'It is to protect legitimate differences and to secure that those differences do not hinder unity.' The fashion in which they manifest the mission of the church in El Salvador will be different from the manner we do in Kansas City; and our way will be distinct from that of the dioceses in Italy, just as Ephesus was dissimilar to Corinth. It has to be that way. And naturally, the style in which you accomplish the Christian mission here, in the urban core, is different from the way John does at his assignment or the way Jim will in his new habitat. Saint Irenaus once wrote that 'uniformity of faith does not call for uniformity of practice'."

"Oh, I like that way of thinking," Sr. Raphael smiled. "It allows us to preach the Good News in ways that mean something special and personal to the people here. It reminds me of what Dr. King said."

She loosely quoted Martin Luther King, Jr., using her own words more than his. "'If the church doesn't recapture her prophetic zeal, it will become irrelevant, without any pull. If the church refuses to participate in the struggle of life, it will cause people everywhere to say that it has atrophied its will.'"

Andy had not said a word yet. He had a tendency to keep his concerns bottled up inside. Often they came out in other ways, at

184

later times – in times that were not appropriate, in ways that could have been avoided.

"Andy," Jim asked him, "What do you think of this?"

Andy cleared his throat and spoke nervously.

"The issue here is the vocation crisis." He looked around at everyone in the room. "We should be talking about how to get more priests to fill this shortage in our Diocese."

Jim, the two nuns, and I hoped that the others would not receive Andy's statement as outrageous, even though it may have been off the mark for this conversation. We knew that he didn't want additional work and might not be able to handle the duties of a parish without some qualified assistance, or some qualified guidance.

Frank, who doesn't know Andy well or any other priest ordained for his own Diocese after Andy (because he has spent the past fifteen years in Central America), did react, but not insensitively.

"Andy, I think the vocation crisis that priests face today is not about numbers. It's about attitudes. Maybe there is a priest shortage. Certainly there is, compared to times earlier in this century here in the States. Certainly there is not, if we compare it to other centuries and other states and nations. But maybe God is offering us an opportunity, here and now, to be better Christians and leaders through what seems to some of us like a shortage."

Sister Raphael jumped in to help Andy.

"I agree with you that what looks like a crisis does demand our response. I think that the proper response from us is to change our ministerial partnerships, our perceptions and misperceptions. If we are going to enhance the Church around here – the mission of Christ – we'll have to call forth a new generation of leaders and provide them with a new set of tools to carry out the unchanging mission which, we know through the Scriptures, God intended."

Jim brought us back to our original objective of discussing a plan for the church's presence in the central city given the reality of fewer resources.

"When we look ahead, we should remember that there's not going to be one correct answer, one correct solution, or one correct direction to go in. With eight of us present, we ought to come up with at least eight good options. We have the capacity to build something wonderful that will form and reform according to the situations we will face in the times ahead of us."

It was at about that time that Vincent, Talib, and DeRon walked in and that I introduced them to all these religious people to whom they would be serving dinner. Ms. Annie, the cook, was ready to get the food going. The boys were ready to earn a few bucks and consume a decent meal afterward.

On our way into the dining room, the Vicar noticed that Andy was uncomfortable. He pulled the high school teacher aside and asked him quietly, "How are you with this potential arrangement, really?"

Andy looked down and said, "Distressed..." Then he managed a smile and added, "...but blessed!" Really, though, he was bewildered by the exchange of those who gathered and by the direction they intended his life to take.

We gathered again at the table. Though ours would not be "Babette's Feast," it, too, would foretell of the heavenly banquet. Gathered around the table, Jim offered our prayer of thanks. His words recalled that Jesus brought his first disciples to the table of fellowship as he brings us in our times. Jim reminded us that Jesus' was a table of justice and peace. His words pleaded for God to help us to call others in our city to the table of fair housing and just salaries, to the table of respectful care for senior citizens and underprivileged children, to the table of racial harmony and Christian charity. He voiced our hope for a place where rich and poor could dine together.

After we sat down, the man in black, our Vicar General, who

was good at politics and leadership, asked, "Besides creating a strategic plan, which we have not yet attained, what additional assistance can your Diocese bestow to help enhance your endeavors?"

That leading question, which rarely got asked in many dioceses, set the tone for the rest of our meal.

In the way that the question was proposed, Frank knew that Fr. Marshall was asking him, too.

"Hugh," he said, "I'm starting to feel more at home here all the time."

Frank doesn't mind visiting Kansas City, but this city is no longer his home, no matter how hard he pretends.

"Four years ago when I was in town, I attended one of these priest's meetings and the big agenda item was whether priests should wear their stole on the inside or the outside of their chasuble when saying Mass. We can't even afford chasubles at Madre de los Pobres. I couldn't wait to get back there. At least, this time, I think you're discussing something worthwhile: how we can best serve God's children. Anyway, no one should serve them, ordained or otherwise, unless those potential servants have given some clear indications of being able to love."

I wondered if I filled that prerequisite.

"And this meal is terrific, too," Frank added.

It was a typical meal from the loving hands of Ms. Annie: barbecued ribs, cornbread pudding, greens and a potato casserole, followed by her famous sweet potato pie. Of course, when Ms. Annie cooked, it was always delicious.

"Sitting here sort of reminds me of what it might have been like when Jesus sat down to sup with Zaccheus or Matthew or Mary and Martha or Simon, people who were part sinner and part saint. Like them, we're just doing the best we can."

I appreciate the way he said that last phrase, "doing the best we can." Every time I hear it, I pray that I, myself, really am.

Although I am nervous about the year ahead and not ready

for Jim to depart, it is Andy who is really concerned. The next day he would tell us – his housemates – that he couldn't possibly take on parish duties in January when Jim is scheduled to report to his new assignment. It is happening too soon for Andy. He complained that he couldn't adjust his teaching schedule for the next semester without more warning. Though we realized that it is just an excuse, we conceded that he needs some more time.

During the next week, the three of us would talk with the Vicar again. We would explain why we need a longer transition period. Such a period would allow Jim to remain till the end of Andy's academic year, and thereby allow Andy more time to get used to the idea. It would also give him time to learn how to work with a pastoral associate who can carry out the day-to-day tasks of whichever parish he inherits. Our brother priests in eastern exurbia will have to be patient, too. Marshall won't like it, but he will learn to live with it and find a way in which everyone involved can live with it.

But our true concern is for Andy who is currently teaching in a school because he didn't think he could handle a parish. He threatened to bail on us once before, and we were concerned that he might try again if this situation is not handled carefully. We all realized, though none said it, that Andy's big apprehension is in forfeiting his summers.

He usually lavishes in the sun for three months and visits retreat centers around the country. Each year he tells Jim and I that he is planning to write a book that will rank the best retreat sites in the United States, sort of like a vacation guide book. But when he finally sat down to write it, he determined that it should be a book of photographs, instead.

"Pictures will tell the story better than words anyway," he proclaimed.

But to this day, he hasn't started this all-important project of which he has done so much research.

One of the good things that many of the priests and religious like about working in the diocese that serves the Kansas City area, is that the managers at the central office try to help their employees at various church sites. Like Fr. Marshall, most of our leaders can adjust. They attempt to make situations benefit all the people involved with them. They are careful about placing appropriate personnel in jobs within the scope of our capabilities and interests.

Like several other bishops, ours assigned a religious woman to work as the chancellor – a position traditionally, though unnecessarily, reserved for priests. And he hired lay leaders to run other major offices, which some other bishops frown upon. They are locked into having no one other than a priest operate such offices. Our Bishop made this attempt to model for his parishes how the laity, religious, and ordained can work together to guide our flocks through the changing climate of Catholic Church leadership.

Oh, he takes some criticism for it. For example, our Diocese got featured in two or three extremist magazines (which claim to be mainstream). Their critical articles were published at about the same time. Though our diocesan leaders aren't particularly proud of the press they received, they didn't mind the criticism because they know it was offered out of ignorance. Besides that, I reason that the people who take time to read those kind of negative articles aren't usually the types who are very good at recognizing God's presence anyway, kind of like those who read the gossip tabloids who are not very good at recognizing the truth. I suspect that our diocesan leaders take such jabs more as compliments, thinking that if narrow-minded journalists such as these single out our local church as an enemy, then we must be doing something right.

When Marshall asked the question "what additional assistance can the Diocese bestow..." there was one response that he expected. And he got it...again.

189

I gave it to him.

"There has got to be something you can do about those "Spirituality Reports" and the statistical data that goes out based on them. Those reports are only concerned with the Catholics who get served by our efforts: time, energy and sacraments. Yet you know that the majority of our time and the majority or our work is spent with non-Catholics. We can't ignore those who are members by virtue of our pantries, our emergency assistance programs, our programs for single-female-heads-of-household, our neighborhood action programs, our senior nutrition programs."

Each year pastors of Catholic parishes complete and return to their diocesan chancery a spirituality report to update officials regarding census information. The report is especially concerned with the number of people attending the Catholic Masses, the number of parishioners receiving the Sacraments, and the number of Sacraments a priest performs in the course of a year.

I was angry that our central office wants to equate the number of funerals I perform in church to the amount of work I produce for it. Most of the funerals I perform are not recorded in our church records anyway, because they're not for church-going folks. Those we work with usually contact us out of crisis and because they don't go to church.

Jim concurred, "It really is unfair to publish that the priests in these parishes serve about three or four hundred households, compared with priests in suburban parishes serving thirteen or fourteen hundred, or twenty-three or twenty-four hundred. Those reports are pretty insensitive to the needs of urban ministries. They only want to know about Catholics, when it's clear that our work reaches more non-Catholics who, by the way, are usually not interested in converting religions. That three or four hundred that we submit could easily be changed to seven or eight hundred to offer a fairer comparison. One of my parishes even honored a non-Catholic as our 'Parishioner of the Year' last spring at our annual recognition gathering."

Frank smiled because he thought that the statistical reports were bullshit anyway. They don't have anything to do with the Gospel's mission. Such reports do not concern him at his primary church, Madre de los Pobres. In Latin America they don't worry about many of the things that worry Catholics north of the border. They don't worry too much about the vows of celibacy there either, sort of like we don't worry about the promises of simplicity here, sort of like they don't worry about the promises of obedience in other spots on the globe.

I added my own exclamation point to the matter.

"We have more people getting emergency assistance each week here than we have worshipping on weekends here. But you can't tell me that we should fold up our tents and move on because they're not Catholics or because they're not self-supporting."

Father Marshall regretted asking the question, but respected our concerns. He probably couldn't do much to change the way that reports get handled anyway, except to perfunctorily repeat our words to someone else. He refrained from responding. I hoped that it didn't sound to the Vicar like sour grapes out in the vineyards.

The chancery official allowed Fr. John to make the summary statement on that hot topic.

"The church needs to be here for the simple reason that everybody else has left. If there are still human beings who need to be served, then we need to be with them. Where the need is the greatest, the church must be its strongest."

With our "business" out of the way for the evening, Frank asked the group: "Don't you all argue about who's liberal and who's conservative anymore? That's been a big topic every other time I've returned."

"No," answered Jim. "I think that one was solved when somebody figured out they are actually the same. A conservative is a liberal who's been named a monsignor; and a liberal is a conservative whose prayer life has instructed him to value all life, not just in the womb...or something like that."

His attempt at humor didn't go over very well.

Andy joined in and tried to help him out.

"I heard a cute definition of a "charismatic" the other day. It's a person who kisses anything that moves, and if it doesn't move, he'll kiss it till it does."

Andy laughed loudly at his own words.

The three teens could hear him from their place in the kitchen. Talib mocked his teacher, saying, "My, that is cute."

"How about this one?" Fr. John tried a different ecclesial definition. "A priest in Texas defined a liturgist as 'an affliction sent by God so that Catholics who have never suffered for the faith may not be denied the opportunity to do so.'"

As the church humor started, Sister Mary Ellen and I decided that it was time to ready the sanctuary, and welcome the penitents of our community. Before we left the rectory, we brought Ms. Annie and the boys, her helpers, into the dining room to thank them.

The guests applauded Ms. Annie. Then some of the priests and Sr. Raphael made a big deal about "her helpers," saying that they ought to become priests and carry on for us in the future.

I could hear Vincent mumble under the laughter, "I don't think so!"

Andy pointed to the boy's younger brother.

"This one is my student. I've been teaching his class that a vocation to the priesthood is a special call to a special soul to a special life of special service to God. I'll tell you, it would have to be divine intervention if he got ordained."

Though Andy laughed boisterously once again, both Frank and Talib, at the same time, rolled their eyes.

Talib isn't the smartest student in school, and he gets into trouble way too much – usually because of his mouth. But according to other students, Father Lucca is especially rough on him.

I told Talib that "it is just because Father Lucca wants you to do your very best and because he cares enough about you to not let you get away with stuff. He cares enough about you to challenge you more than he does your classmates."

Talib didn't buy it, though.

He had a different theory. One day during the summer I had sent Talib from the church on an errand to our house to get a book for me. While there, the boy ran into Andy who had been lounging out in the backyard of our house. As I've been told the story, Andy had his Barry Manilow music cranked rather loud on his "walk-man," and he was wearing nothing but some tiny speedo trunks and a pair of sunglasses. It got back to him that Talib said he was "undressed and unblessed." The young man was only having fun with the scene, but he probably shouldn't have said anything to other students. But, as Vincent says, "my brother just talks too much."

The three teenagers thanked all the priests and nuns for saying nice things to them. Their mother instructed them to always say "thank you" even if they don't mean it, so that they'd never get caught meaning it, but forgetting to say it.

Fathers John and Jim walked over to the church together. Jim thanked him, again, for driving in and being part of the meeting, as well as for staying for the prayer afterward.

"I don't mind this role I play in our Diocese," John answered. "I am a minority in all things. I'm a man in a time that favors women, a priest in a time that favors the laity, and a celibate in a time that favors intimacy. If you remember, I chose to be a black leader in a mostly white church. No, I really don't mind at all."

On Reconciliation

4

As our Reconciliation Service began, the choir burst into a song about hope.

> *" ...There is hope!*
> *When they've scandalized your name*
> *There is hope!*
> *Don't worry, don't be ashamed*
> *There is hope!*
> *Lift up Jesus' name*
> *And put your trust in Jesus*
> *Let Him have His way*
> *There is hope for your today..."*

During the service, Sister Mary Ellen talked to the parishioners. Lots of them were present to listen. She told us that it is each member's duty to build up our church community because it is each Christian's duty to build up God's kingdom. She told us that since so many black folks only pray when they're in trouble, "God lets us get in trouble all the time." She said that we've got to work our way out of the trouble; that together, and with God's help, we will find our way.

She told us that the meeting before dinner reassured her that the Diocese will be close by to support us, but we will have to stop our bickering.

"An eye for an eye," she instructed us, "will eventually make us all go blind. It's not necessary to blow out somebody else's light when you want your own to shine. They'll shine brighter together, and together we can find us the way."

Then she read the Beatitudes from the tax-collecting evangelist's fifth chapter, while the pianist played some soft music, undertoning her proclamation of Jesus' teachings. She read it like poetry. When she finished she said, "And let me add one more, from Mr. G.K. Chesterton. He said, 'Blessed are the cracked and the broken, for unto them the light of God will enter.'

"Tonight we are the cracked and the broken," she said after a deliberate silence. "But the light of God will shine on our community if we let him in. Don't be petty and don't pretend that our need for prayer and reconciliation isn't about you. It's about each of us. Don't put your heads down and look the other way when you see trouble coming your way. Don't pray that your life will be made easy. Pray that you will be made stronger, more courageous, and more faithful so that you can face the challenges of your life...and face them with truth and dignity."

Sister told us that, while other people go to see the priests to receive forgiveness, the rest of the assembly should go to one another, too, to ask for forgiveness. Some of the people did, but not the president of the Women's Club or the president of the Altar Society or the man who is a Parish Council officer and who doesn't trust priests. But some of the gossips did, and so did Sister Mary Ellen. The evening's prayer would help some of the tensions around here, but it wouldn't solve them.

Vincent, Talib, and DeRon sat near the back of the church, close to where Andy was stationed. He had the longest line of any of the priests. People like to go to him when they confess and ask forgiveness. He never challenges adults, only children. The boys could hear him tell each person who confessed to him to "resolve to evolve." Andy thinks that those words sound better than the traditional departing line: "Go and sin no more." He says it with his arms outstretched so that he can hug the penitent, whether he knows that person or not. And then he reaches out to the next one and does the same act. His line of penitents was also the one that moved the fastest. Maybe that's part of the reason it was the most popular.

A drunk wandered in as the last penitents were confessing their shortcomings. The drunk made a scene, calling out for the pastor. I didn't notice him, but Fr. John who was near the back on the opposite side from Andy, did, and he took the man outside to talk with him. Such people are usually looking for a handout.

The scenario is almost routine around here. If persons ask for money because they need food, we always offer them food instead of money. If they ask for money because they need a ride somewhere, we always offer them a ride instead of the money. I will take them myself, when I can, or we'll give them a bus pass. Such people usually refuse the food and the ride, which makes us think that they actually only want the money anyway. I don't carry money because beggars rarely use it for what they say they need.

Vincent knew that scenes like this are not unusual. He and his brother followed the two outside, just in case the beggar would cause some trouble for Fr. John. He didn't. But even if he did, Fr. John could have handled it.

Once I heard about a famous person who converted to Catholicism near the end of his life. When asked why he had done so, he responded, " ...because I desired to be forgiven."

In a society in which people are driven to beg, I suppose that

196

we ought to desire to be forgiven, too, by each other and by God.

As we concluded our prayer service, we knew that we had experienced forgiveness, confession, penance, absolution, healing and indeed, reconciliation. The choir sent us home as they had earlier united us.

"There is hope!
When all else is gone
There is hope!
When it seems like everything's gone wrong
There is hope!
Remember in this song
To put your trust in Jesus
Let Him have His way
There is hope for you today..."

When I gave the three teenagers a ride home that night, I noticed the full moon hanging low in the sky. It didn't seem as dark as it usually does at nine o'clock. But to me, the darkness in the neighborhood where we live is always somewhat eerie. There were people sitting inside of cars, parked on either side of the streets. They use the vehicles as if they were another room of their house. There were kids standing in the streets acting as though they weren't going to allow my car to get past them. Old men with whiskey bottles in their hands were sitting along the curb. It is stuff like this that makes it seem eerie.

"More eerie than a graveyard," I had once said to Vincent, "and almost as eerie as a monastery."

It's interesting to me that during that conversation about scary neighborhoods, Vincent informed me that his neighborhood doesn't frighten him as much as white neighborhoods.

"The so-called nice neighborhoods give me the creeps more than ours does, Father. There's hardly any action going on in them. When black kids go into them, drivers slow down and watch us, or make a move for their car phones; curtains and blinds in the surrounding houses get pulled back, and lots of calls get made to the security companies that patrol their areas. I wouldn't want to live in those kind of neighborhoods. They're more eerie than ours."

Some of the unique features of our neighborhood are almost charming, or at least interesting. One phenomenon, which intrigues me, is the ringing pay phones and the neighbors who hang around them waiting for calls. I had never heard a pay phone ring before I moved to the inner city. Twice I answered ringing pay phones. The first time I was surprised when the caller asked for a particular name, but more surprised when I called out the name and a person with that name came out of a doorway about five yards away. The second time I answered a pay phone, I got propositioned by a woman who said that she was watching me as we talked to one another. I haven't answered another ringing pay phone since.

Frank rode with me to take the boys home. The two of us were talking in the front seat; the kids were messing around in the back. I didn't realize that Vincent was listening to us, but he was. In a subsequent conversation several days later, Vincent told me that what I said to Frank stunned him and made him conclude that maybe I didn't believe in God.

That's not what I said. What I said to Frank was that before I became a priest, I grappled over signing my oath of office, which is a prerequisite to getting ordained.

"My spiritual director in the seminary told me finally, 'Oh just sign the damn thing – you agonize too much over simple things.' I didn't think that it should be a simple thing: the Creed, fidelity to the Pope, accepting the statements of the Church as truths. On one level, I believe it all. But on another, it seems so distant from what I'm doing, that it makes my doubt seem greater than my belief."

Frank responded, "There is certainly a chasm between Rome

and El Salvador. Thomas, you're like I was, trying to make sense of the discrepancies. Except I stopped agonizing a long time ago. That's not the kind of stuff worth our agony. If you can believe in what you're doing, then the rest is going to take care of itself."

"I've just been thinking that maybe I shouldn't be the leader of a group when I can't buy into their rules," I told him.

"Why did you sign the "Oath of Fidelity?" he asked.

Each priest, before he gets ordained to the transitional diaconate, the final step to the presbyterate, makes a pledge to uphold the Creed and teachings of the Church and Pope. With his left hand on the Holy Bible and his right hand raised, the future priest promises to remain faithful always. Then he signs a paper signifying the promise, known as the "Oath of Fidelity."

"Two reasons really. And I truly didn't think that I was deceiving myself with either one of them, at the time. The first was because my spiritual director, who knew most of my hang-ups in detail, gave me his approval. And the other was because I am so amazed that God chose to become one of us. It is so unbelievable to me that something inside tells me that I have to believe it. And if I believe it, I determined that I'd have to do something radically drastic with my life to show that I believe."

"Is the Incarnation the center of our faith, or is it the Resurrection?" Was Frank being sarcastic again? I couldn't tell.

My response was hesitant.

"For me, they can't be separated. Stuff has happened to me which causes me to conclude that maybe one time in a billion or so, unbelievable things do actually happen...walking through walls, time travel, communion with other worlds, walking on water.... I think that somehow, then, just one time in a kazillion – one time in the entire history of the universe – God could and would become one of us."

I pulled my car over onto the side of the street in front of Vincent and Talib's house. DeRon was going to stay overnight with them.

Before they had gotten into the car at the church, I gave them fifty dollars for helping serve the meal. Fifty is difficult to split equally among three, but I like to hear how they work out things like that. I usually give them money even though our parish struggles to pay our bills, even though they probably should be volunteering their time. But my gestures are efforts at exposing them to some good church people – efforts at motivating them to imitate the generosity that they witness, and efforts at encouraging them to do better things with their own lives. That is my hope. Some criticize such generosity, protesting that it feeds a dependence mentality, which creates even more dependence.

"Thanks a lot, guys!" I said. When I next saw them I would want to hear what messages they took from the Reconciliation Service. I often call on them to articulate some facet of what they learn by sharing it with me or with some other person or group.

"Oh yeah, Vincent," I added, "I almost forgot to ask, how's it going with Aimee?"

Aimee is the girl who was in church the month before, the one over whom his brother made such a big deal. Talib had caught up to her after that Mass – the one in which I preached about the wild grapes – and told her that Vincent wanted to ask her out, but was too shy.

Here's how Vincent told me the story: "I thought about killing him three days later, when he told me what he did. But he was right. I did want to ask her out, and I was too shy. I guess she told him that if I really wanted to go out with her, I'd have to overcome my shyness and just ask."

Vincent ran into her two weeks later at a shopping mall. He was going to a movie with a friend and she was shopping, buying something for her grandmother, as it turns out. The young man was embarrassed, but he mustered up enough nerve to talk to her. He wouldn't have done it if she had not been alone. And he wouldn't have done it if his brother had been with him, either. He told his friend to get the tickets and that he'd be right back.

So he walked over to where she was shopping. They made a joke about Talib's big mouth. Yet it was his big mouth that ended up getting Vincent his first date with her – and two other dates since. She lives over in Kansas, but it's not very far really. She visits her grandmother, who lives within a mile of Vincent's house, so they plan to see more of each other in the future. She's a very nice young lady.

"Just fine, sir," Vincent answered, as he stepped away from my car.

"Good," I smiled.

The back windows on the car were rolled down. I would customarily wait till the kids got inside the door, even though they warned me that I was probably in more danger than them when I did so. When Talib and DeRon opened the front door, I continued my conversation with Frank.

"It may sound strange to you, but that's why I signed. I'm not sure what I believe, but I know it's possible for me to believe all of it...and you're right, I sure do believe in what I'm doing."

We drove away into the rest of the evening.

As we guided our way back to our priests' residence, I wanted to hear more from him. Frank had been invited by Jim to stay the night with us.

"Why did you decide to escape to El Salvador?"

"I used to hate that question," he hesitated, "but it's a fair question."

He paused again.

"I don't know if I was running to or running from. Probably both. The bishop at that time asked for priests to volunteer for many things – experiments really – while the Council's documents were starting to get implemented. Lots of guys were choosing one thing or another. More international relationships were being encouraged. Our two dioceses attempted to partner. I knew a little Spanish, but that really wasn't a factor. I was working in the Chancery as the vice-chancellor. Lots of younger priests had titles like that. They meant nothing. We were apprentices of sorts, learning the system from church government bosses who wanted it all kept inbred. I remember being overwhelmed by all the bullshit that went on there. Most of the big shots were liars and cheats. They sucked up to the bishop, and he let it happen. My boss, the chancellor, Jack Kroll, was the biggest bullshitter on the whole diocesan staff. He embellished like an Irishman and lied with a poker face. Each day I'd come in, sit there, listen to all his bullshit and divide everything I heard by five, and then I'd go out and talk to others like I was some badass myself!

"I kept thinking about a Latin phrase we used in the seminary: 'Illegitimus non tantum carborandum.' Maybe you used it too...'don't let the bastards get you down.' Then I realized that I had become one of the bastards, creating all kinds of sticky red tape and all sorts of heavy red cable, creating work for others that was so worthless. I had to get out. El Salvador provided me the distance I needed to revive my commitment to God and his people. You're right, it really was an escape. It has been my salvation. I don't know what I'd do if the Bishop told me to come back to Kansas City. Don't think I could do it. My heart has shown me a home a million miles away. I've come to realize that Christianity, my kind of Christianity anyway, doesn't do very well in affluent societies."

He paused again, and then added, "All those years of studying Latin...and it's the only phrase that did me any good."

When we got inside the house, we sat up for a while with Jim. Frank told us, again, that he enjoyed the evening and was happy to have been part of it. He opened a small bottle containing what he claimed was wine from El Salvador. I didn't know that wine was made there. Though the two of them drank it, I passed on the offer. I never could stand the taste of wine – any wine. The priestly ritual at Mass, letting the consecrated drink pass my lips, is a sacrificc.

"It's this kind of struggle and reconciliation that reminds me that this work is worth me trading in my life." Then he asked the question, "But where are all of our fraternal jackasses I usually see up here?"

"Oh, they're still around," Jim responded. "We only let you see the good guys this time."

They were referring to members of our diocesan presbyterate who make life difficult for their "brothers in the Lord." Some are jealous, some have grown mean, some still jockey for positions of power, some use their work to strengthen their status, some simply cannot see things from a viewpoint other than their own. Those last ones are probably the ones to whom Frank was making reference.

He added, "I've often learned that when Catholics look for God, they look to priests. I hope they're not disappointed most of the times they do. As the great Mark Twain once wrote, 'Religion is a dangerous thing, unless you get it right.'"

"Are you disappointed with the priests you know?" I asked him.

"I've met many of them who had rather pathetic lives," he admitted. "And I think they joined the church because, it is here they reasoned, that they'd encounter lives even more pathetic than their own. It's not the majority, but too many just the same."

"I can see how our position could cause some priests to feel better. It's a position of bonding with people instantly, couseling them, even judging them. Though it's not our intention to judge them – at least most of us – it's a position of great power. Sure it can make some guys feel good," Jim offered.

"In a sick sort of way," Frank added. We agreed.

Jim spoke again, "I've noticed a change in recent years, maybe because we've accepted the fact that we priests are a dying breed.

In spite of the jackasses, I think we've put out some real measures to support one another. I guess we discovered that the alternative didn't work."

For a while we spoke about some of the priests who had helped or hindered our images of priesthood. It seems that Frank didn't have the same kind of luck that Jim and I did on getting assigned to a good first pastor who might teach him the compassion of Christ to accompany the "truth of the church's teachings."

Old Monsignor Schweiger, Frank's first pastor, took his young curate to the parish school to introduce him on his first day of priesthood. Their first stop at eight o'clock in the morning was the first grade classroom where, in his gruff voice, Schweiger interrupted the sister's lesson to teach the class some religion "like their parents paid for." Between coughing spells, he accused the five and six year olds of "staining their souls with the blood of Jesus." The old man, who frightened Frank as much as he did the little ones, pointed at the children, and with the wrath of a madman, let them have it. "It is because of your sins that our savior died," he accused them. "Repent and seek mercy for what you have done!" Frank told us of how some of the little children started to cry, though none of them had any idea why the "sick old man" was carrying on. Most of them had trouble staying inside the lines when coloring. They didn't need this, too.

Though we sometimes laugh about such clerics as characters of our profession, we agreed in our disgust of these characters that got away with far too much power. When we agreed that such abuse of power is rather disgusting, we stopped laughing.

Finally Frank noticed that Andy wasn't with us, and asked about him. Andy had been in bed for over an hour, by that point. We pondered whether or not he could handle the combined schedules of school and parish. Jim decided that he'd better bring up the subject to our housemate again, the next day, to make sure.

Even though we had gone over this inevitable course for the Central City with him several times, Andy still appeared to be very confused by what transpired earlier in the evening.

As Frank noted, "he looked more perplexed than a Jesuit during Holy Week."

The result of a future conversation with Andy and a subsequent agreement with the Vicar General was that Jim would end up remaining with us for eight more months. I am glad that he would. Even more than Andy, I am glad. In those ensuing months LaChance would help me get through several difficult times: the death of a long-time pantry volunteer, the rape of a young neighborhood girl, and my processing of how God calls me to love others more deeply.

Oh, how I long to love others more deeply.

The Cross and The Road

5

My mother scolds me occasionally because she doesn't think that I defend the faith publicly as well as I ought. When she says such things, I know that by "publicly" she means to include my conversations with other priests and co-workers as well as my discussions with family members and friends. Clearly she wants me to seek the truth. And she trusts that all truth is held by Holy Mother Church.

Like her, I recognize my obligation to represent the Church and the oath I made to it. But unlike her, and others of her generation, I, like others of my generation, recognize a clear distinction between God and the Church. Some of us also sense the sham involved in upholding a public stance that doesn't reflect one's private views. And I now realize a truth of the mystery of God contained in the inner cities of which the Church in Rome appears to know little.

I want to learn the truth about God and the Church as it's revealed to me. It's revealed to me by priests like Frank, dedicated religious types like Sister Mary Ellen, and good people like Dorthea. Then I want to pass it along to younger Catholics like Vincent and other children like Reaundra Jenkins.

I was thinking about my mother, and the lessons she taught me, and those she still wants me to learn, as I listened to the words of the young man speaking to me. Vincent was telling me what he recently learned from the Reconciliation Service and from some of the events that led up to it.

"What you and Sister were telling our parish was that, if we remain indifferent, then our world can never become any different. Our society can't afford to be indifferent about violence and crime and drug use now, just like Martin Luther King's society couldn't afford to be indifferent about prejudices, injustices and forms of slavery back when he was alive.

"I learned that if I am going to be different, I can't be indifferent," he reported.

We didn't have this follow-up conversation until the week of Thanksgiving, but I still wanted to have it. I am interested in what facets of religion impact him and other young people.

"What does that mean for you, Vincent?" I asked him.

"It means that I stay on the straight and narrow. My grades are mostly A's and I'm going to have to keep them that way if I'm going to be accepted into a good engineering college next year."

Basketball season was starting, and his coach told me that Vincent would have a good chance for a basketball scholarship too...if he stays focused. But the boy didn't mention basketball to me. He didn't probably because he knew that although I think sports are great for young people, I don't want any of them to count on sports as a way to a better life.

"Some of my friends booze it up, but I know I don't need that stuff," Vincent continued with his recitation of what it means for him to be different. "I really like Aimee, and she likes me, but we can't do anything stupid to mess that up."

He was referring to sex, and presumed that I would track his message. When in one of his serious moods, he shared with me that he had only had sex one time before. He meant with one girl, but several times. He said he realized that they were lucky that she didn't get pregnant or that one of them didn't spread some horrible, deadly disease to the other one.

"I sure don't want to die or be a father...yet," Vincent said. Then he added that he wants to be a dad someday, but not for many years.

"Ever since that first day I talked to you, I have wanted to be right with God. That's what makes me different from the dope heads and the gang bangers. Not becoming indifferent means that I won't let people I care about screw up their lives either," he concluded.

After a quiet moment, I spoke.

"I certainly wish you well, Vincent, but I suspect that your different way won't always be easy."

"Oh, I know that, sir." He didn't want to give me the wrong impression. "It won't be easy at all."

"This prayer might help you," I said. I handed him a little booklet entitled *The Way of the Cross*. "It helps me to stay focused. Do you know what it's about?"

"I'm not sure, Father," he answered hesitantly, though I knew that he connected it with the fourteen pictures on the sidewalls of the church. Sister Mary Ellen had explained the pictures to Vincent's Confirmation class as they walked around and even prayed at each of them during one class period.

"When you read these words and pray this prayer, you'll be reminded that Jesus tried to stay on 'the straight and narrow' too. He tried to stay focused on God, just like you try, because he was clear about what his goal was, just like you are."

Vincent wasn't aware that Jesus' last walk had anything at all in common with the choices he was making about school, girls, sports, drugs and friends. Perhaps it didn't, but I choose to think it did.

"What do you mean when you say you think this prayer might help me?" he asked.

"Well, the way, or the road, is a kind of symbol for life. A Christian life needs to be focused on the goal of taking the way that leads to God. That means choosing the right road, over and over again.

"Some good people and some bad people got in Jesus' way. The crowd harassed him, the soldiers beat him, and the government leaders turned the other way, giving license to the mob.

"They were indifferent.

"A man named Simon helped him, though he was pressured into it. A young woman named Veronica stood up against the mob and comforted him. The older women, who knew and loved him, offered all that they had: their tears and their prayers...not much, but all that they had." I paused before continuing. "I think that's sort of like our lives."

"You mean the good and bad people who are along our way can either help us to stay focused or distract us?"

"Maybe even destroy us," I added. "In this prayer, Jesus falls three times. I think he did that for us. Along the way, we're going to fall three thousand or three million – maybe even three billion times. Those are the mistakes we'll make."

"But the way of the cross seems to travel in a different direction from the way of hope that you keep preaching to people is going to save us," Vincent argued. "You don't want us falling and making mistakes, do you?"

He was right. I did talk from the pulpit often about not losing hope, especially in the times when we lose some of our faith or lose our sense of love.

"Vincent, I think I learn the most about myself through the mistakes I make, in the times that I fall. And I fall a lot. By falling, Jesus showed that he was one of us. By getting back up, he showed us that we can be one like him.

"Every time you attend Mass," I continued, "the priest says 'he partook in our humanity so that we can share in his divinity.' I think that means that when we fall, like men, we've got to get back up, like gods. We've got to be focused on carrying Christ for others, because Christ was focused on carrying the cross for us. I think that to journey in the way of the cross is to travel in the way of hope and walk in the steps of Jesus. Our city streets aren't all that different from the city streets of Jerusalem. Does that make any sense?"

"Yes, sir. It makes some sense." After a brief pause that seemed much longer because he stared at my face, piercing me with his eyes, he added a question.

"Father, can I ask you something?"

"Of course," I responded.

"As a priest, do you think you're following that road, or the way, of Jesus?"

"Not very well, maybe, but I'm trying."

I was sincere in my answer. I wanted to convey to my young friend that we should each do our best to follow the one we profess saved us by that path he took.

I continued. "Vincent, I suppose my path as a priest seems more like Robert Frost's 'Road Less Taken.' Do you know about that?"

He shook his head.

"Frost's poem," I explained, "tells of struggle involved in making life's choices. He describes standing at the two roads that diverged in a wood and debating whether to follow the well worn way or the grassy path that wanted wear. He finally stated his decision this way: 'and I, I took the one less traveled by, and that has made all the difference.'"

I briefly outlined for him my struggle in choosing the priesthood as well as my internal debate about serving in the urban core where I sometimes don't seem to be effective or appreciated. Though I didn't say it to him, I reflected that there aren't many young men lining up to enter seminaries, and among our priests, there aren't many asking to live in the inner cities.

"My road of priesthood and way of following the Lord right now is to walk these streets around here," I concluded.

"But you're still walking them, Father. You're still following him. When you try to follow the road of Jesus, it seems like you end up taking the one less traveled by. And you're still finding your way, so it must be making a difference to you somehow."

He was right. I made a choice. Once we make choices, it's sometimes difficult to stay on the chosen path. But that is the essence of the prayer that I had only recently handed over to him.

"I'll pray the prayer," he added, as he got up to leave. "And I'll ask God to help me stay focused...especially when it won't be easy."

"I hope it will help you. Maybe you can get your brother to pray it, too. He's not as strong as you, and he will fall a whole lot more."

He wondered if I knew about Talib's drug dealings in the past, or about the girl he'd been fooling around with lately.

"I guess when we fall, we've got to find enough reason to stand back up, right Father?"

"Right," I smiled. "And not only that, Vincent. If we can muster up enough strength and faith and perseverance to do so, we'll discover that we'll be standing a step ahead of where we were before we went down. We'll be one step closer to our goal."

Vincent was forced to listen to me unload quite a bit of religious verbiage on him in our periodic talks. Some of it probably made sense to him. Some of it probably didn't.

He told Sister Mary Ellen that "it seems like the Father's dad or somebody else who helped him grow up, told him all this stuff and now he has to tell his own son. But since he doesn't have a son, he has to tell me because I'll listen."

"Vincent," I concluded, "I'm proud that you want to be different. Treat yourself with respect. Treat your girlfriends with dignity, too. Keep improving on who you are and you'll influence others to do the same. I hope more young men will follow the road you're choosing."

And I hoped it would make all the difference for him.

After we finished talking – that is, after I finished exhorting (or unloading) and he finished paying attention, I began going through my busy routine of returning phone calls, confirming meetings, responding to mail, and attending to the concerns of the volunteers and staff members.

Then I sat down to think about my old deceased friend, the wonderful Monsignor from my initial and formative days as a priest. Like Jesus, Monsignor O'Hara poured out his blood for his people...not literally, but truly. Every time that beloved pastor picked up the chalice of wine at Mass, he offered himself for the sake of those whom he had been sent to serve. Those grapes really did turn to blood – picked, smashed, pulverized, stomped upon, and poured out for the people.

I know that in his priesthood, Monsignor O'Hara had, at some time, moved from immature love to mature love, from romantic love to real love, from easy love to difficult love, from self-centered love to other-centered love. I envy his notion of love and regret my loss of enthusiasm to pursue it.

I began to wonder how Monsignor celebrates the Eucharist in heaven. Then my thoughts turned again, and I wondered if O'Hara's vineyard at Mary Immaculate was really any less wild or untamed than my own at St. Peter Claver. I doubt it. Monsignor just knew how to handle it, or to let Someone else – "the mystery we call 'God'" – handle it.

In each of the final days of his life, as he lay there unable to move, the worn-out Monsignor asked me to read to him the story of Jesus' passion. And it always had to be the same rendition from *The Gospel According to Matthew*. I have no idea why he needed to hear that particular translation so many times at the end of his earthly life.

The only difference from the other Gospel accounts, that stays in my head, is Matthew's telling of how the bodies of the saints left their tombs and roamed around, appearing to people who recognized them.

Besides telling LaChance, I didn't tell anyone about Monsignor's ghost roaming around. Yet I knew it had something to do with the roads I walk and the cross I bear; it had something to do with my search for God, my search for truth.

Moving On

6

Christmas Eve was less than a week away. Though I appreciate Advent's spiritual value, I was anxious for the holidays of Christmas, Kwanzaa, and New Years to arrive. Among the festive celebrations, liturgical gatherings, and continuous parties, the part that I like best is that for almost two weeks, I would be freed from evening meetings – a practical value. But on the first night of winter, there were enough to last me through the New Year.

There were, in fact, three meetings taking place at St. Peter Claver on that particular night. I shuffled around to each of them and pretended to be interested in their agendas.

But I was actually spending my evening attempting to conjure up a clever and profound way to retell the Christmas story in the days ahead. While I was listening in on the Worship Committee meeting in the sacristy, a woman, still young but very tired and worn-down, burst into the Catechumenate meeting which was taking place in the Church Hall below us.

She called out for the pastor: "Where's Father Thomas?"

Though she called me by name, she had never seen me before. Someone instructed her to go upstairs to the church's sacristy.

Upstairs, a committee member was talking about how we could get some Christmas trees donated since the person who was supposed to acquire trees for the church's decorations this year fell through on her commitment. The committee seemed to make a bigger deal out of it than what I thought it deserved. So I was sitting with them thinking about George Bailey in Bedford Falls, the Grinch in Who-ville, and Ebenezer Scrooge among the poverty of 19th Century England. At the same time I wondered how we would get enough donations to produce Christmas baskets for the three hundred households in our neighborhood that expected them.

As I sat, I was thinking about Christmases past, present and future. Mine were thoughts of anticipations and thoughts of disappointments. They were thoughts of hopes and of fears for future ages. They were a distraction from the meeting and I welcomed them until I welcomed the woman who barged in to take away this precious time that I was wasting.

When she came to me, I could tell that she had obviously been beaten up recently. Her left eye was swollen and colored. The whole area around her cheek and jaw was disfigured. She tried to cover them up with cosmetics, but the make-up didn't do its job. She wore a cast on her right wrist and hand.

"Can't you please help me?" she sounded desperate.

"It depends on what sort of help you need," I responded, trying to get sensitive, while trying not to get taken.

"Let's go out there, so we won't disturb everyone here."

As the Worship Committee members watched, I accompanied the woman out of their sight into the church's sanctuary where I could give my full attention to her request and where she might feel respected more than pitied.

"I need money for a cab."

"We don't give out money. I don't carry any cash on me."
I have learned to be clear and firm in my responses to beggars. I
noticed her old, tattered coat, and the fact that she wore no hat or
scarf with it. Though it wasn't freezing outside, it was still cold.
She should be dressed warmer if she was walking. Is that why
she wanted the cab?

"I've walked here from 55th and Landhigh. I don't need much
money."

She had walked between four and five miles, not an easy walk
either. I dread the part of town of which she spoke. It is much
worse than my own, always so dark and dirty. Sidewalks are
cracked, corroded and covered in mud. Streetlights are shot out,
traffic signs are torn down. Dangerous road hazards are often in
the streets. Nothing ever seems to get repaired there. Maybe the
city fathers think: "why bother?" Trash and garbage gets dumped
anywhere there, everywhere there. Some of the St. Peter Claver
parishioners live in that area. I know it well.

"Why did you walk so far?" I asked, then added, "And when
was the last time you ate something?" I meant to keep that last
thought to myself, but it must have found form out loud.

"I ate yesterday," she responded first to the question which
was far more important to her. "My two kids are hungry, too."
She then responded to my first query. "I stopped at four other
churches. No one would help me. Finally somebody at that learning center up the street said I should come here. They said you'd
help me."

I don't usually appreciate that kind of advertising, but I certainly would search for a way to help, if she really was in need.
So many people are really in need, but I suspected that she was
desperate.

"Let's go next door and get you something to eat, and you
can tell me why you need a cab."

Scrooge must have been in a fog, still, as he moved with the Ghost across the hall that led to the door at the back of the house. As the door opened, and he saw the lonely boy reading by the feeble fire, he must have felt distraught. It was then that "Scrooge sat down...and wept...wept to see his poor forgotten self as he used to be," as Charles Dickens told it. I thought about the ghost of his past, the ghost of his first dream. When he asked, "What is the matter?" Scrooge, through his tears, could only recall the little poor boy who had sung Christmas carols at his door the night before, the little boy whom he told to get lost. He must have recalled the child's state in life, his poverty, his desperation.

"He recalled all of it," I thought, "and regretted that he had given the child nothing. No sign that he cared at all."

I know that a look at the truth is a difficult look to take. But that's the look that John the Baptist wanted people to take in preparation for the Messiah. John's desert was retold in Scrooge's darkness. John's roar was retold through Scrooge's restlessness. John's chaos was retold by Scrooge's Christmas Eve. If Dickens' character could discover the truth of his own identity, I thought that so should Christians discover the true identity of John. He was a reflection but he wasn't the light. He was a voice but he wasn't the word. He was a saint but he wasn't the savior of humanity. He was there to announce the good news, announce that we could repent and be saved. It isn't too late for us...yet.

By walking with the woman, I was walking with mystery and suffering, with another poor, forgotten soul that hopes for a Savior.

As we entered the rectory, located only thirty feet from the church, Dickens' story reminded me that some ghosts will haunt us into redirecting our lives for the good so that we can better comprehend our mission.

Sister Mary Ellen and the Social Outreach Committee were to have a light meal at their meeting, held in the rectory's space.

The meeting was necessary because they needed to go over some final plans for distributing the three hundred Christmas baskets we were to offer needy families. Though the meal had ended by the time the woman arrived to interrupt the three meetings, I was certain that there would be leftovers.

I made a plate for her and brought it to the small kitchen table, separated from the meeting. There we sat together. Mindful of the other events I was missing, I recalled something that Monsignor O'Hara had told me: "Don't get angered by the interruptions to your work. The interruptions are your work."

She ate, though not very much. And she drank several glasses of apple cider, then asked for some water. As she did so, she told me about her plan to escape from her abusive husband during the night ahead. She couldn't take food home to her children, or her husband would realize that she hadn't gone where she said that she must go: to the school of their older child, for a parent-teacher conference and a group meeting. She was sure that he wouldn't show his face at the school and also wouldn't restrict her from going.

The woman proceeded to tell me about her ordeal. She is from Indianapolis. Her family still lives there. She doesn't know anyone in Kansas City. Her husband doesn't allow her to have any relationships outside of his home. She is allotted no financial allowance, no hobbies or interests, no personal life, no life at all except the one that serves his needs. He beats her regularly and, as she told it, he recently beat their children, too. It was because of this recent act that she became scared.

His mother lives with them. And the mother thinks that her son does no wrong. His mother criticizes the woman for not satisfying her son and for raising two rotten children.

The woman and her children would be catching the bus to Indianapolis at four o'clock in the morning. She already had the three one-way tickets. She didn't tell me where she got the money to buy tickets. And I didn't ask.

She had been to a police station already that evening. The officer with whom she spoke agreed to arrive at her husband's house at two o'clock. At that time, they would charge him with domestic violence. The officer told her that she would have to get to the bus station on her own, for the police can't offer such rides. But they would make sure that she could pack some things, and that, along with her children, she could leave the house safely.

I had never heard of pre-arranged responses to domestic violence calls. I would contact the officer at Central Patrol with whom she met. But it wouldn't surprise me, if it were true. I had witnessed unorthodox police behaviors when I was on a police "ride-along" two years earlier. Officers harassed young black men without apparent reason, they created action when things were slow, they randomly pulled over cars when they didn't like the looks of particular drivers, they pointed their guns at law-breakers. I suspected that there certainly could be some eager volunteers for an early morning tangle with a woman-beater.

I clearly did understand how officers have to protect themselves and one another, and I understand how angry they become when one among them gets injured or killed by a bad guy. But I am struck by how much some cops seem to enjoy the part of their job that permits them to harass the criminals and potential criminals. It seems odd, but some of the police officers I've encountered and some of the criminals I've encountered have similar personalities.

Though the woman couldn't bring food home to her children, she agreed to wrap some cheese squares, hide them in her coat, and let her young ones eat once they were out of the house, and freed from their future past.

It would cost them eleven dollars to ride in a cab to the bus station, but she had no money for that singular part of her escape plan.

At the first church in which she stopped, she was told that they don't give money to people who are not members of their faith community. So she walked on, heading onward to another, then another, and another. Most of those churches were locked up for the night, but at the ones where pastors or deacons were on hand, they delivered to the woman other reasons why they could not give her eleven dollars.

She told me that she would have a life, and that her children would have a future in Indianapolis. She told me that, although she had left her husband before, this time she really meant it. How many times I had heard that before!

After she had eaten, I gave her a twenty dollar bill which I retrieved from the cash box in my office, then offered to take her back to the place from where she came. I was deeply touched by the sadness of her story, by the distortion of her appearance, by the limited hopefulness of her children's future.

As we got into my car, I thought about Clement C. Moore's telling of the night before Christmas, how "the stockings were hung by the chimney with care in hopes that Saint Nicholas soon would be there."

I considered how the author's telling of Santa Claus was similar to Advent's telling of Emmanuel. "Emmanuel" reminds me that God is with us. But would the woman and her children know anything about that? Anything about Advent? Anything about Emmanuel?

In December, everyone wants to welcome Christ, everyone wants to be Santa. They want to recreate the magic of giving so they remember and reach out to the sick, the elderly, the handicapped, the poor, those who get forgotten during the remainder of the year. I appreciate the fact that I, and the woman who came to see me in the night, were given this lesson on giving and receiving, for it is the primary lesson of the season.

As we drove from the parkway onto other streets, which led to side streets, I was aware that the night was very dark. And as we rode, it got darker. There were fewer streetlights, fewer house lights, fewer Christmas lights.

The woman asked me to slow down in front of one particular house that didn't fit the pattern, a house that refused to let darkness overcome it.

"It looks brighter than Las Vegas," she said, though she had only seen pictures.

As I pulled the car over in front of the house, the woman began to cry. For the first time during the entire evening, she cried.

"I think that's the most beautiful thing I have ever seen in my life," she stared up at the house. She thanked me there in the car, as she had in the kitchen, as she had in the sanctuary. "No one would help me, and you helped me."

Christmas lights were blinking on the roof, around the windows and doors, on every tree and bush, and along the sidewalk that led up to the house's front door. There were illuminary statues scattered around the yard – of Joseph and Mary and the baby Jesus, of an angel, of three reindeer, and of the jolly little man sitting in his brightly-lit sleigh.

I blinked my eyes, trying to clear my vision. It was not a sleigh; it was a fiery chariot. And it wasn't Nicholas inside, nor was it Elijah who stepped into a sleigh of fire and flew into the sky never to be seen again. To the children who listened to the myth of Christmas stories and Bible stories through the ages, those two never died. "Odd, isn't it," I thought. Monsignor O'Hara, holding the reins from his place in Santa's seat, looked back at the two of us as we stared up at him. Our car remained parked on the side of the road for what seemed like a very long time. We simply looked and admired the beauty of the lights.

"...And what happened then? Well, in Who-ville they say, that the Grinch's small heart grew three sizes that day!"

I was searching for a story of the Incarnation, one like the

221

songs that spark the magic of the season, one like Dr. Seuss' classic that gets to the guts of true faith and offers reason. With each block, I drove deeper and deeper into the dirt and filth of my hometown, into the heart of the Christian mission, into the ugly world into which Christ was born.

The woman asked to be dropped off several blocks from her short-term destination. As she opened the car door to walk away, into the black night, she told me, "Everything is gonna be all right now..."

It seemed like she had a need to convince me of it. It was she who consoled me. "...Everything will be just fine."

I sure hoped that she was right. But at this point in time she was so disconnected that she couldn't even afford a welfare Christmas for her children. I prayed that their bus ride to Indianapolis would be a ride to a better life. From the disorder of the darkness of the night ahead, two children and their mother would seek some share in the mystery that remains at the heart of the winter solstice now upon them.

Frosty, Rudolph, Santa and all the rest simply mythologize the greatest story of them all, the story of when the angel of the Lord appeared in the middle of another dark night saying, "Fear not...I bring you good tidings of great joy...for unto you is born a Savior."

I watched through my rearview mirror as she walked in the other direction down that cold, dark and lonely street. I watched her until she faded from my sight.

Growing Up

7

At about four thirty, one January morning, the phone next to my bed rang. It startled me. Calls at that hour usually mean trouble and heartache.

"Yeah, this is Fr. Hartigan." My voice was guttural and groggy.

"Father, I need your help," the voice on the other end came back at me.

"What's wrong?"

"I'm in jail. Can you come get me?" I recognized the voice. It belonged to Talib.

"Are you hurt?"

"No. I'm okay. But I don't wanna go home. They said they could release me to you if you'd come."

He wasn't in jail, really, but his situation was almost as bad. He was being held at the Metro Patrol police station. Some of the cops there know me and are aware of the work that our parish does in the neighborhood. They hoped that I could help

"straighten out" the boy. It was way below zero on this morning
and I didn't want to get out of my warm bed. But I did.

When I got to the police station twenty minutes later, I found
out that Talib had been hanging at some of the bars over on the
Avenue. Though he looks older than his sixteen years, he doesn't
look older than twenty-one. But the young man could easily talk
his way into getting served a few drinks. Actually, he can talk his
way into anything. The bar's manager should know better.

Two police officers who were answering some other call in
the area stopped in the bar because, I guess, there wasn't enough
going on outside to keep them busy. Or maybe they came in to
get warm. They saw the sixteen-year-old, who tried to hide from
them. But by that time, Talib was slow to think and slow to
move, because he was high on crack and drunk on Colt 45. The
police wanted to harass the manager, which they did. And Talib,
making a stupid move as he sometimes does, started to fight the
cops.

"He should be in jail," I told them. "I'm not sure I want to
take him."

Then I asked the officer in charge of the holding area, "Is
there a place where I can talk with him?"

I meant in private.

I wished that someone else had received the phone call instead of me. Talib would have called home, but one of his parents would have answered the phone, and that would have made
the situation worse for him. His parents might not have permitted him to be released. Talib used his savvy in this situation. He
was smart to put me in the middle of it.

Talib sobered up enough between one and five o'clock to '
know that he was in serious trouble. But he still looked horrible.
After we got inside the small room and closed the door, I said,
"I'm serious about what I said out there. I think you ought to
spend a night or two in jail. And I don't mean in this nice place...

224

in a real jail."

"I know I messed up," Talib said.

"What happened?"

Talib told me how he went to a place a few houses down from his own to buy drugs from an old man who always maintains a big supply, and at cheap prices. It is the "crap of the crap," as the locals refer to it. Everybody around is aware, even Talib. He told me how distraught he had been nine hours earlier, and how one thing led to another thing.

"But why did you go down there in the first place?" That's what I meant when I asked him "what happened?"

His eyes hadn't looked up at my face since the moment I arrived at the station, but his head certainly went down to meet his eyes when he answered this time. "I got a girl pregnant."

"Oh hell!" I overreacted. "When did you find this out?"

"Last week."

"You haven't told anyone?"

"Nuhuh," he shook his head.

"Did the girl just find out?"

"She's s'posed to have it in two months."

It was difficult for Talib to talk about the whole situation, but he knew he didn't have a choice.

"Have you been seeing her these recent months?"

"No. She said she didn't wanna see me!"

"Well, that's understandable. Does she want you around now that the baby will be here soon?"

"She dudn't. But her dad says we gotta get married or he's suin' me for paternity or somethin'."

"Does her father live with her?"

"No!" The sharp response almost squealed from his mouth. He was nervous and mad. "He has assault and battery charges against him by the mom. He's not allowed to go there."

"How old is the girl?" I asked.

"Same as me."

225

Same as him meant the same grade, not yet half way through high school, barely old enough to have a license to drive a car, not yet mature enough to make rational decisions.

"What does her mother think of the situation the two of you are in?"

"Her mother wants her to stay in school, and she wants to raise it for her."

Without knowing the girl in question, it had not occurred to me that she might have considered an abortion during any time in these recent months. Like some other Catholics who buy into the "seamless garment" theory, I think that because our society tolerates abortions, we are able to tolerate every other unnecessary atrocity that plagues us. I am proud of what the tiny, frail but spunky Mother Teresa asked the President of the United States: "If we accept that a mother can kill even her own child, how can we tell other people not to kill one another?"

Teenage pregnancy is an issue that captures, for me, one difference between the black inner city and the white suburban areas. Though it's clearly stereotyping on my part, it seems that the black girls are proud to become mothers. They know that to do so, they will get to love a human being more than they've ever loved anyone before, and they'll get to be loved by a human being more than they've ever felt loved by one before. Black girls know that a baby is a message from God that the world should continue on for a little longer and that they have a role to play in the creation.

The white girls talk about how abortion is wrong and murderous and all that, but it is usually the first option that they consider, even the Catholic ones. They say they don't, but they do. Their second option is to schedule a wedding, whether they really want to marry the guy or not. Blacks get married for some bad reasons, but children usually aren't one of the reasons for them to do it. Talib's girlfriend's dad's demand is an exception to the norm.

226

But anyway you look at it, Talib had fallen under the weight of his cross, and he just needed to lie there for a while before getting back up. I had explained it to his brother this way: "In the end, Vincent, you'll discover that the only true sin against humanity, and the only true crime against Christianity, is to decide to give up, to not get back up when you're down, laying under what seems like the weight of the world."

I was beginning to think that maybe I had wasted words on the wrong brother. Or maybe Vincent had let me down by shirking his fraternal responsibilities. Either way, I know that Talib makes his own choices, and that he would need some help to stay focused on his goal, whenever he could decide what his goal would be.

But where was Vincent last night, when his brother was all alone, getting trashed, sinking fast and needing a brotherly hand? Vincent and his team played an away-game at a larger, classier high school than his own located across the state line against a highly favored opponent. And he played the best game of his life. He dominated in the lane offensively and defensively, muscling his way for rebounds and finding ways to the hoop many times, inspiring his teammates to also play better. Coach let him stay on the court for most of the game. Everything went right for him, even his outside shot had the touch which landed him a few three-pointers.

After the game, he and some teammates and friends celebrated their victory at a nearby fast food joint. Aimee joined the party. Her role was more of an onlooker than that of a central character. She was Vincent's girlfriend. And she was happy to have that role, both at the gymnasium and the restaurant. Vincent was uncharacteristically talkative as he and his friends recapped the game, joked about their future in the NBA, and even rapped a few songs.

She watched and listened and laughed. In between scarfing

down three cheeseburgers, he interacted with his buddies and kept bringing Aimee into the circle of his friends. He was only recently comfortable letting her into his world.

With not much of a voice or desire to ham it up anymore, Vincent remained seated as much of the activity turned to standing and dancing around the tables which the group had claimed for their celebration. He and Aimee, in the midst of the surrounding commotion, suddenly found themselves alone. At one point, and in between bites, he leaned over and kissed her. They spoke to one another with glowing smiles, unable or unwilling to hear any of the noise around them.

Where was Vincent last night, when his brother was all alone, getting trashed, sinking fast and needing a brotherly hand? He was somewhere in a state of grace; it was a place of happiness.

In the quiet center of the chaos, he told Aimee why he was so happy. It wasn't because he had scored nineteen points, twelve assists and nabbed fifteen rebounds. It wasn't because she was in his life – though that was part of it. They shared a relationship special to each of them in which she opened up for him a whole new world of beauty and possibility.

He was happy because he had finally come upon a mountaintop in his life. He realized that his perseverance and commitment to a positive way of being was paying off. He told Aimee that he had made the decision to attend college after graduation. Even if he didn't have the money and the outside encouragement to do so, he knew that he possessed the skill and brains and inner drive to succeed, to remain faithful to his destiny. He told her that he would be meeting with a college recruiter the next day and he, unlike anyone in his ancestry, would figure out a way to attend college. He was so happy simply because he realized for the first time that he had it within himself to figure out a way.

And he knew that she was joyful for no other reason than that he was happy.

By six thirty, Talib was released into my hands. And I would not wash my hands of him – not yet, anyway. I telephoned his parents from the police station. I then spent the rest of this drab, dark, foggy, freezing morning taking Talib to talk with his mother at home and then with his dad at work. I called the school and ended up dropping him off there by late morning.

The young man would have the tougher and longer-lasting jobs. He, along with the girl, would need to determine his role and responsibility in their child's life. He would need to develop a relationship with the girl's mother and develop a resolution with the girl's father. He would need to devise a strategy for coping with difficult situations (that wouldn't involve the old man down the street or the bars on the Avenue), and dealing with his now-established police record.

Though I shouldn't have joked about it, I suggested at one point in the morning that maybe his Confirmation service hours could be transferable for community service. A judge would probably assign him some of those, too. Talib had many things to think about. I don't know if I could handle what he will have to handle.

It was nearly eleven thirty when I took Talib to school. When he got out of the car, it was the first time in the last six and a half hours that he looked me in my eyes. He spoke very softly, unlike usual.

"Thank you," he said, and he closed the car door.

I had served as a Simon of Cyrene for him, bearing the load of his worries for a brief time. But now the weight of the burden is back on his young shoulders.

I tossed in a cassette tape for the short ride to St. Peter Claver. A rock group from Georgia, REM, was singing "It's the End of the World As We Know It" and I cranked it up loud. The enjoyable noise provided a perfect silhouette for my drive home. I could hardly see the streets against the low, heavy fog. I thought that the music fit well with my view of our neighborhood, a neighborhood from which I was protected by my vehicle, later by my rectory, and always by my Church.

Inside the school building from which I just departed, Vincent spoke with a college counselor and faculty advisor. They talked through the papers stacked upon the table between them. The young high school senior realized that he was at a crossroads in his life. And he was determined to take a step in the direction that no one in his family had yet traveled. He knew that his decision to attend college would demand many personal sacrifices. Though his parents and friends would encourage him onward with their words, their actions wouldn't necessarily follow. He understood that, ultimately, he was on his own.

The war against poverty has many battles. They are fought primarily on the field of education and during the hours after schools dismiss for the day and adolescent crime and mischief are at their height. With numerous setbacks, minor victories may not seem like much. But in my mind, Talib's setback would be overshadowed by Vincent's victory.

It is my religious conviction that all the setbacks of all the youth of all the streets that surround me will be overshadowed by the cumulative victories of hope like the one brought about by Vincent's decision to attend college. For it is his commitment to break the cycle of despair that has enveloped him since the day he was born. He will pass through this crossroad down a path of hope.

Alone Never Again

8

When I pulled into the church parking lot, I could see two figures about ten yards away standing at the door to the food pantry. Even from that distance, I could tell that they were shivering. They were a woman and a young girl, who I recognized as a mother and daughter who came to the pantry on several occasions.

"They must really be in desperate need," I thought.

I was certain that they had walked all the way from their house located near the expressway – six or seven blocks from the church – and on such a frigid morning like this one.

Then it dawned on me who they are. And my heart went out to them. I didn't know them primarily as pantry clients, users of our gracious social outreach. I knew them primarily as wounded people of God, searchers of peace. The woman's oldest child had been tragically shot and killed in the last year or two.

The story circulating at the time told us that her dead son had been mistakenly identified by one gang as a member of their rival gang. But we, in the neighborhood, heard another story that some member of Adrian's 27th Street gang wanted him to be hurt and scared. But nobody knew why. The dead boy, Ronald Jenkins, had never hurt a soul in his life. He really was a good guy – stayed to himself, mostly. I spoke at his funeral at Sister Mary Ellen's urging because his family didn't have a church of their own – only ours – where they came for assistance to help them through emergency situations.

I got out of my car quickly. I wanted to catch up to the mother and daughter to say something to them – anything. I wanted, so badly, to help make their existence better. But by the time I got out, they were already inside the basement door. Through the thick air I could see Dorthea, our gracious pantry volunteer, step out into the cold to let them enter before her. She and Sister Mary Ellen were very good for the mother and daughter. She did everything possible to encourage the sorrowful mother, and she kept trying to reach out to, and encourage, her poor young daughter, whose name I couldn't remember, nor pronounce.

When I realized that I had missed them, I stopped, frozen like a statue. And in my stupor state, I said a prayer to God through blessed Mary, recalling the sword that once pierced her heart. I looked down and saw a drop of blood on the ground by my feet. It lay frozen in a patch of snow left from another day.

My prayer was for the young girl, especially, because I was flooded by my recollection of how sad and confused she looked when I last saw her. And my prayer was for her mother, and for the babies, who were probably abandoned at her home again. So many children are forced to care for themselves early in their lives. I prayed that the little ones would have a future. I prayed that the mother would suffer no more.

I prayed that the winter would yield to spring. I prayed that death would yield to life. I prayed that springtime would bring new life to this vineyard which I hope has poured out its last drops of blood.

A hundred and fifty years ago when the time was right, Harriet Tubman, inspired by Harriet Beecher Stowe and Abraham Lincoln, sparked the revolution that was needed to wake up a nation. Fifty years ago when the time was right again, Rosa Parks, inspired by Martin Luther King, Jr. and Robert Kennedy, sparked the revolution again – and woke us up again. But who would spark the revolution for the next generation of black Americans? The time seems right for a new revolution. Perhaps some little girl, like the Jenkins' child, will grow in age and wisdom and mercy, to become another great woman, a woman on the horizon, who can wake us to what's important. For our society has fallen asleep once more.

In their walk through the morning, shrouded by the blistering chill of the biting wind and the heavy fog over the darkened neighborhood, the mother and daughter walked by faith more than by sight. They walked their journey in the very way that God's word instructs each of us to walk.

I wished that I could catch a glimpse of the neighborhood surrounding us. I wanted to see it, right at that very moment, to reach out and touch it, like I could almost touch the captured clouds. Isn't there some kind of light that can dispel this darkness? I know that something will rise up from the chaos of its formless waste. Will it be revolution? Or will it be resurrection?

I recalled a voice that I had heard recently in the night, the voice of my dear, departed friend which told me: "Worry not about what lies dimly in the distance. Concern yourself with what lies clearly before you."

As I stood a few feet from my car, looking in the direction of the closed food pantry door, the only structure that I could see clearly was the rear of the church, which towered right in front of me.

"If the doors of perception were cleansed..." I thought to

myself.

Then I recalled how Moses begged God to let him – a mere human – see him, God Almighty, just once. God told the man that no human could look upon God and live, for such a gaze would be too much to behold. But because they were so intimate, Moses persisted. Finally God said that he would let Moses see his backside. I supposed that the story intended humor...or that creation, itself, even a neighborhood like ours, was the backside of God. That is sort of humorous, too.

It's not too much to behold, but maybe it's enough to let us know that some part of God is among us. Either way, the backside of God gave Moses the hope and the confidence that he needed to carry out his mission. I hope that the backside of the church structure could do the same for me.

I need some hope and confidence now because it might convince me of how God mysteriously cares for the people.

I need some hope and confidence now because it can keep the members of our community going, in spite of our trials, confusions, questions, fears, loneliness, bad news and doubts.

I need some hope and confidence now because, as St. Peter wrote, "the hope and promise of our inheritance can never be spoiled...can never fade away."

I need some hope and confidence now because I want to look into the future with joyful, optimistic hope and the confidence of being able to co-create a better world. If only I could discover a little light within, I can help illuminate the way for others.

So I stood there in the cold, like a statue. And I prayed that the little ones would have a future and that the mothers would suffer no more.

"We boast of our hope...as we boast of our afflictions. We know that afflictions make for endurance, and endurance for tested virtue, and tested virtue for hope. And this hope will not leave us disappointed."

– Romans 5:2-4